Edward Hayes Plumptre

A Popular Exposition of the Epistles to the Seven Churches of Asia

Edward Hayes Plumptre

A Popular Exposition of the Epistles to the Seven Churches of Asia

ISBN/EAN: 9783744762014

Printed in Europe, USA, Canada, Australia, Japan

Cover: Foto ©Lupo / pixelio.de

More available books at **www.hansebooks.com**

THE EPISTLES TO THE SEVEN CHURCHES.

A POPULAR EXPOSITION

OF

THE EPISTLES

TO THE

SEVEN CHURCHES OF ASIA.

BY

E. H. PLUMPTRE, D.D.,

VICAR OF BICKLEY; PROFESSOR OF DIVINITY IN KING'S COLLEGE, LONDON;
PREBENDARY OF ST. PAUL'S.

New York:
E. P. DUTTON & CO.,
713, BROADWAY.
MDCCCLXXVIII.

CONTENTS.

I.
INTRODUCTORY 1

II.
THE EPISTLE TO EPHESUS 53

III.
THE EPISTLE TO SMYRNA 87

IV.
THE EPISTLE TO PERGAMOS 105

V.
THE EPISTLE TO THYATIRA 133

VI.
THE EPISTLE TO SARDIS 155

VII.
THE EPISTLE TO PHILADELPHIA 173

VIII.
THE EPISTLE TO LAODICEA 193

I.

INTRODUCTORY.

I.

I DO not purpose entering on a discussion of the authorship or date of the Revelation which claims to have been written by John the Divine (ὁ θεολόγος).[1] I accept the all but unanimous tradition of the writers of the ante-Nicene Church that it was the work of the

[1] The title thus given to the Apostle claims, however, a few words of notice. The view commonly taken by Patristic writers and modern critics that it represents his special character as the special witness of the incarnation of the divine Logos ("the *Word* was *God*") is, of course, probable enough in itself and has much to recommend it. It should not be forgotten, however, that it may have had a local starting-point. The researches of Mr. Wood (*Ephesus, Theatre*, p. 23) have brought to light inscriptions connected with the great Temple of Artemis which shew that this very title was given to the highest order of priests consecrated to the service of the goddess. They were pre-eminently the *theologi*, or divines, who unfolded to the worshippers the inner meaning of her *cultus*. The name may therefore have been at first the embodiment of the thought that the Evangelist occupied in the service of the true God the position which they occupied in that of the Ephesian goddess, that he was the witness of the Truth, of which her worship was the counterfeit, and could tell men how and through whom the Eternal had manifested Himself both through nature and among men.

beloved disciple, partly because the tradition in this case is sufficiently early (A.D. 170) to have something of an historical value (I refer especially to the Muratorian Fragment), partly on account of the internal coincidences of thought and language, on which I have dwelt elsewhere.[1] I hold, with not a few recent commentators, that it belongs to a date earlier than that of the persecution under Domitian, to which Patristic tradition for the most part assigned it; that it was written certainly before the destruction of Jerusalem, probably during a time in which the Asiatic Churches were suffering from the persecution of which we have traces, as affecting that portion of the Empire, in the Pastoral Epistles (2 Tim. i. 8, 15; ii. 3; iii. 12), yet more definitely in the First Epistle of St. Peter (i. 6, 7; ii. 12; iii. 14-17; iv. 1, 12-19), and in that Epistle to the Hebrews which I have been led to assign to the same period.[2] The Neronian persecution was obviously more than the effect of the cruelty or policy of an individual tyrant. It was only possible through the excitement, the suspicion, the hatred, which pervaded men's minds in the imperial city as they found them-

---

[1] *Bible Educator*, i. pp. 27, 79.
[2] See papers in the *Expositor* on "The Writings of Apollos," vol. i. pp. 329-348, 409-435.

selves face to face with the power and life of the new society that bore the name of Christian; and that hatred and suspicion were as certain to be felt in every city of the Empire as in Rome itself.

About this period, then, probably shortly after the death of Nero (say *circ.* A.D. 68 or 69), John, who speaks of himself—as Paul (Phil. i. 1) and Peter (2 Pet. i. 1) and James (James i. 1) had done before him—as the servant (δοῦλος, *i.e.* the slave) of Jesus Christ, dropping the name of apostle where there was no pressing necessity to assert his authority as such, wrote the book to which he prefixed the title of Revelation. Exceptional as that title now is among the Books of the New Testament, we must remember that neither the word nor the thing were exceptional in the apostolic age. It was by " visions and revelations of the Lord" (2 Cor. xii. 1) that each Apostle was carried forward from truth to truth and received fresh insight into the work he had to do. In this way Stephen had seen the Son of Man standing at the right hand of God (Acts vii. 55, 56), and Peter had been taught that the gate of Eternal Life had been thrown open to the Gentiles (Acts x. 11), and Paul had been carried up to the third heaven and the Paradise of God (2 Cor. xii. 1-4, 7), and had from time to time beheld the form of the risen and ascended Christ (Acts xxii. 17, 18; xxviii. 9), or of some angel sent by Him (Acts xxvii. 23). In this way prophets and apostles had been taught what till then eye had not seen nor ear heard, neither had it entered into the heart of man to conceive. (1 Cor. ii. 9, 10.) Each mystery of the faith was imparted by a new revelation. An apocalypse extending to the far future, to the coming of the Lord, to the signs of its approach, is implied as given to St. Paul in 2 Thess. ii. 1–12; in 1 Tim. iv. 1–3; and to St. Peter in 2 Pet. ii. 10–13. It would hardly be a paradox to say that a state commonly so abnormal as that of trance or ecstasy was part of the normal life of the Apostles of the Faith. John, when he addressed his Revelation to the Churches of Asia was claiming no exceptional privilege. They would not be startled by it as by something altogether extraordinary.

The writer describes himself further as one "who bare record" (ἐμαρτύρησε) "of the Word of God and of the testimony" (μαρτυρία) "of Jesus, and of all things which He saw" (i. 2). I cannot bring myself to confine the application of these words to the contents of the Book to which they are thus prefixed. The Apostle had, for some greater or less length of time, been working and preaching in these Asiatic Churches, and describes himself as having done a work which they would recognise as truly his. If we accept the Fourth Gospel as either being by St. John, or as, at least, representing the characteristic features of his teaching, we note that the idea of witness, record, testimony, is throughout the keynote of that teaching. When the spear pierced the side of Jesus, " he that saw it bare record, and his record is true" (John xix. 35). He closed his Gospel with the declaration, " This is the disciple which testifieth of these things and wrote these things " (John xxi. 24). I do not, of course, assume that the Gospel was written before the Revelation, but I infer from the prominence given to the word μαρτυριά and its cognates, alike in Gospel, Revelation, and Epistles,[1] that it had all along been characteristic of his oral teaching, and that that teaching is referred to here. And, assuming this, I cannot hesitate to see in " the Word of God " to which he bore witness more than the spoken Message of the Gospel. He who beheld in Christ the " Word made

---

[1] The word " witness," in its noun or verb form, is found not less than *seventy-two* times in the writings ascribed to St. John. It is pre-eminently his characteristic word.

flesh," who, even in the earlier stage of thought to which the Apocalypse belongs, saw Him who was faithful and true, on whose head were many crowns, who was clothed with a vesture dipped in blood, and whose name was called THE WORD OF GOD (Rev. xix. 11-13), was not likely in his opening words to use that name in any lower sense than when he wrote after wards that, " In the beginning was the Word " (John i. 1), or that the " Word of Life " was that which he had seen with his eyes, and had looked upon, and his hands had handled (1 John i. 1).

And he writes to the Seven Churches of Asia. What chain of events brought the Apostle to that region we know not. The silence of Scripture is nowhere more remarkable than in connection with the period of his life from the time of the Council at Jerusalem (Gal. ii. 9) to that in which we find him as an exile in Patmos. All that we can say is that it is probable that the sacred charge of watching over the mother of his Lord kept him for several years in comparative seclusion, and that he appears to have left Jerusalem before St. Paul's last visit there, and not to have arrived at Ephesus when the last extant Epistle of that Apostle was written to Timotheus. We can, however, form a fairly full picture of the state of things which he found on his arrival, and which probably had drawn him thither that he might fill up the gap that had been left by the departure or the death of the two great Teachers to whom these Churches had till then looked for guidance. A time of fiery persecution, of fierce outrage, and foul calumnies; a time also of sects and schisms, evil men and seducers waxing worse and worse, deceiving and being deceived; the polity and discipline of the Church thrown into confusion; the teaching of St. Paul forgotten, or, worse still, exaggerated and distorted; the very teachers and bishops of the Church becoming the leaders of sects and schisms,—this is what we find portrayed in the writings which must have preceded his arrival (on the hypothesis which I have adopted as to the date of the Apocalypse) but a few short years or months. And the storm of persecution falls on him also, and he finds himself at Patmos. The tone in which he speaks of himself as being there "for the sake of the Word of God" (I do not abandon the higher sense even here) "and of the testimony of Jesus Christ" (i. 9) suggests the thought that he had been banished there by some judicial sentence. Rejecting, as unsupported by any adequate evidence, the tradition that that sentence came from the mouth of Domitian, or of any other Roman emperor, I fall back upon an assumption which is in the nature of the case far more probable, *i.e.* that he had been condemned by some local authority, most probably by the Proconsul of Asia, who had his seat at Ephesus; and I find in the comparative leniency of the sentence as a substitute for that death, which fell on so many believers elsewhere, even in the Asiatic Churches (Rev. ii. 13), a token of the continued influence of those who, like the Asiarchs that were friends of Paul, and the town-clerk of Ephesus, were so far favourable to the Christian society as to be unwilling to join in violent measures for its extirpation. (Acts xix. 31, 37.) There is no proof, so far as I know, that Patmos was at 's period one of the ordinary places of deportati though it is true that any one of the Cyclades or Sporades might have been chosen for this purpose, and so far as the Book now before us suggests an inference it points rather to solitary exile and comparative freedom. There is no trace of the *custodia* of a state prisoner, no indication of chains, or of sentinels in guard over him.

At such a time the thoughts of the exile

would naturally turn to the Churches from which he was thus for a time separated. He would know the excellences, the trials, the perils of each. They would be prominent in his anxieties and prayers. He would crave to know what were the right words to speak at such a time to his companions in tribulation. The Churches to which he is told to write were, perhaps, actually those with which, and with which alone, he had been personally connected; but it is also possible that the habit of his mind was to group whatever was presented to it under definite numerical relations; and that the number Seven, so full of sacred and mystic meaning, the symbol of completeness and of calm, seemed to him to include all the chief types of spiritual life with which he had been familiar. Certain is that that number is nowhere more prominent clothed with mystic meaning than it is in this Book. Over and above the seven golden candlesticks and the seven stars which correspond to the Seven Churches, we have the seven lamps of fire (Rev. iv. 5) and the seven Spirits before the Throne (Rev. i. 4), the seven seals (Rev. vii. 1) and trumpets (Rev. viii. 2), the seven thunders (Rev. x. 3) and angels (Rev. xv. 1) and vials (Rev. xv.); the beast with the seven heads (Rev. xii. 3), the seven mountains (Rev. xvii. 9), and the seven kings (Rev. xvii. 10). The seven Churches thus chosen were accordingly for him the types and representatives of the whole family of God. It may be said, as our induction from the seven messages will shew, that there has never been a Christian community, flourishing or decaying, exposed to the dangers of persecution or prosperity, that may not find its likeness in one or other of them.

And to these Churches he writes with a salutation which the Epistles of St. Paul had made familiar—"*Grace and peace*"—and which, so far as we know, had been used by none before him. Men felt that it was truer and deeper than the old χαίρειν of the Greeks in either of its senses; more full of meaning than the "Peace" which had been the immemorial greeting of the Hebrews. (Luke x. 5.) It brought with it the truth that "grace," the favour of God, was more than joy, and was the fountain of all peace; it did not suggest, as χαίρειν, like our Farewell, had come to do, the idea of parting. In any case it is interesting to note the fact that St. John, to whom both the other greetings must have been familiar in the Church at Jerusalem (Acts xv. 23, and James i. 1), throws himself thus freely into Pauline phraseology.

If I mistake not, even this coincidence, trivial as it may seem, is at least of some weight against the theory of some recent critics,[1] that the Apocalypse is a polemic anti-Pauline treatise. The individuality of the writer asserts itself, however, in the words that follow. It is not, as with St. Paul, "Grace and peace from God our Father, and the Lord Jesus Christ," but, "*from him which is, and which was, and which is to come*,"—or, as the Greek has it, with a singular disregard of the technical rules of grammar—ἀπὸ τοῦ ὁ ὢν καὶ ὁ ἦν καὶ ὁ ἐρχόμενος.

It would be idle to ascribe this departure from usage to any ignorance of those rules, and to infer from it the early date of the Apocalypse, as written before the Galilean disciple had become familiar with the language in which he wrote. It is clear that the Apostle looked on the Divine Name, though it took the form of words that admitted of inflection, as having a character as sacred as that of Jehovah or Adonai had been in his mother tongue, not losing its majesty by changing its unapproachable loftiness. The LXX. translation of Exod. iii. 14 had made ‘O ὬN ("He that is")

[1] I may name M. Renan as the ablest and most distinguished advocate of this theory, in his "L'Antechrist," pp. xxix. 34.

the Greek equivalent for the I AM of our English Bible; and that was, therefore, naturally the first word in the strange compound which the Apostle formed to express the Eternity of God. But that Eternity, that Ever-present Being, might be thought of as stretching into the infinite past and the infinite future, and two other names were wanted. The Greek verb of being, however, had no past participle, and therefore he had to fall back upon its imperfect tense, "the He was." It might, of course, have supplied him with a future ὁ ἐσόμενος, but from that word he turned aside, partly, it may be, because it would have suggested the thought of *coming into being* at some future point of time, partly because Hebrew phraseology had led him to find the thought of futurity in the verb "to come." And so we have ὁ ἐρχόμενος, " he that cometh." It is possible that the familiar "he that cometh" of the Gospels (*e.g.* Matt. xi. 3; xxiii. 39), applied by the Jews of Galilee and Jerusalem to the expected Christ, might have helped to determine the choice of that word; but the distinct mention of the Christ himself in the next verse forbids us to refer the word even remotely to the thought of his second Coming to judge the world. The one idea which the Apostle strove to embody was that of the Eternal Now, as contemplated in the time before the world, and as it shall be when God shall once more be all in all. If St. John uses a familiar phrase, it is as with a significance altogether new. It is scarcely possible to think of this Divine Name without remembering that inscription so strangely like, so yet more strangely different, of which Plutarch speaks as being in the Temple of Athene (the Egyptian Isis) at Sais: "I am all that has come into being, and that which is, and that which shall be" ("Ἐγώ εἰμι πᾶν τὸ γεγονός, καὶ ὂν, καὶ ἐσόμενον), "and no man hath lifted my veil." Alike in contemplating the mystery of existence as spreading through the infinite past into the infinite future, they differ in all else as widely as any two creeds that the world has ever seen. The one, in its identification of God with the universe, in its postulate of an "Ever-becoming" instead of an Eternal Being, in the absolute exclusion of personality by its use of the neuter form of the participles; in its assertion that the Deity thus described is the Unknown and Unknowable is the despairing creed of the Pantheist. The other is the proclamation of the name of One who is not only the I AM THAT I AM (Exod. iii. 14), but the Everlasting Father, revealing Himself through his Son. Is it altogether too bold a conjecture to suggest that the contrast between the two formulæ was deliberate and designed? The inscription at Sais was, we know, from the way in which Plutarch speaks of it, at this very time one of the familiar topics of many religious inquirers. Was it likely to have been unknown to the Alexandrian Jew who had recently been at Ephesus, mighty in the Scriptures, and not unversed, as a scholar of Philo, in the lore of Heathenism? Is not the contrast between the ὁ ὤν and the πᾶν τὸ γεγονός identical in character with that so sharply drawn in the prologue to St. John's Gospel, between the self-same verbs, "He *was*" (ἦν) "in the beginning with God," and "All things *were made*" (ἐγένετο) "by him." (John i. 2, 3).

In the next words we have a yet more marked individuality. St. Paul nowhere joins the Spirit with the Father and the Son in the opening salutation of his Epistles. The nearest approach to such a combination is found in the well-known words of blessing of 2 Cor. xiii. 13, " The grace of our Lord Jesus Christ, and the love of God, and the fellowship of the Holy Ghost, be with you all." The use of the three Names, however, in the formula for Gentile baptism (Matt. xxviii. 19), which by this time must, to a large extent, have superseded the earlier or Jewish form, " In the name of the Lord Jesus" (Acts ii. 38; viii. 16; xviii. 8), must have made it natural to use them in benedictions, as they were shortly afterwards used in doxologies; and we may add that the order in which the Names were to be used was shewn, by St. Paul's example in the words just cited, to be a variable one. We are startled, however, by a yet greater variation. He speaks not of the one Holy Spirit, but of "*the Seven Spirits which are before the Throne.*" Why, we ask, should he, who so distinctly records afterwards, and must even now have remembered, the teaching of the Lord Jesus as to the One Spirit, the Paraclete, the Comforter, bring in here the idea of plurality? The answer is to be found, in part, in the nature of the visions which he proceeds to record. He had seen "the seven lamps of fire burning before the Throne" (iv. 5), and the seven eyes of the Lamb (v. 6), and had learnt to see in each of these the symbol of the Seven Spirits of God, as representing in their completeness all gifts of illumination and insight that are possessed by God, and are communicated to man. That imagery rested on the older symbolism of a prophet whom the writer of the

Revelation seems to have studied devoutly. In the visions of Zechariah also there had been seen the seven lamps, or branches of the one lamp (Zech. ii. 2), the seven Eyes of God (Zech. ii. 9; iii. 10), as symbols of his eternal Light and all-embracing Knowledge. But the genesis of the symbol carries us yet higher. In the passage in Isaiah (xi. 2) which had most impressed on men the thought that the Messianic King was to be filled by the Spirit, there were found numerically seven spiritual gifts, each described as being an attribute of the One Spirit of the Lord. As an influence nearer to the Apostle's own time, and traceably operating in other instances (as, *e.g.*, in that of the LOGOS) on his thoughts and phraseology, we may note the fact that Philo also speaks of the number seven in its mystical import as identical with unity, as unity developed in diversity, and yet remaining one.[1] The Seven Spirits were, therefore, under such conditions of thought, the fit symbols of the diversities of gifts bestowed by the one and self-same Spirit, dividing to every man severally as He wills. (1 Cor. xii. 11.)

It was to be expected that one who had first learnt to know God in Christ, the Father through the Son, should reserve the fulness of

---

[1] Philo, Bohn's Translation, i. p. 145.

his thoughts and speech for Him whom he had thus known and loved. And the words in which his thoughts find utterance are every way characteristic. For him the first great attribute which attaches to the name of Christ is that of "*the faithful witness.*" That was the thought which had been prominent in the personal teaching of his Lord as recorded in his Gospel. He had come into the world to bear *witness* to the truth. (John xviii. 37.) He testified that which he had seen and heard. (John iii. 11, 32.) Though in one sense He did not testify of Himself, but of the Father, yet the works which the Father had given Him to do bore their *witness* of Him. (John v. 36.) But this thought also attached itself to divine words of earlier date. In the very prophecy which, as speaking of the "sure mercies of David," had come to be looked on as essentially Messianic (Acts xiii. 34), as the sequel to the invitation, "Ho, every one that thirsteth, come ye to the waters," which is quoted by St. John himself in this very Book (Rev. xxi. 6; xxii. 17), we find the character of the coming Christ portrayed as one who is to be given as "a *witness* to the people" (Isaiah lv. 4). In the Psalm, which had in like manner acquired a like significance, the reign of the future King was described as that of one who should be as the "faithful *witness*" in heaven (Psa. lxxxix. 38); and if those words referred, as they have been thought to do, to the "bow in the cloud" as being, like the moon in her vicissitudes and her sameness, the ever-recurring token of the stability of the divine promise, then "the rainbow round about the Throne, in sight like unto an emerald," of Rev. iv. 3, may well have recalled the very words (ὁ μάρτυς ὁ πιστὸς in the LXX. Version) which had been used of it by the Psalmist. But the Christ is also "*the first begotten from the dead and the Prince of the kings of the earth.*" The reference which we have just traced to the great Messianic Psalm explains in part these words also. If that Psalm had been present in its completeness to the writer's memory, he would find there that it was said of the divinely-appointed King, "I will make him my first-born" (πρωτότοκος, LXX.), "higher [1] than the kings of the earth." More noticeable still is the fact that the very words now used by St. John had been used before by St. Paul (Col. i. 18), and that we must therefore infer either that the name had come, through the

---

[1] The Hebrew for "higher" is Elion, the word used for the "Most High" of the divine name, so prominent in many passages both of the Old and New Testament.

teaching of that Apostle, to be familiar to all the Asiatic Churches, or that the Disciple, who has been sometimes thought of as representing a different section of the Church and a different phase of teaching, deliberately adopted a title which St. Paul had used before him. But it must be remembered also that to him the words came with a special significance and power. He had seen his Lord after He was risen. He had heard the words, "All power is given unto me in heaven and earth" (Matt. xxviii. 18). He had witnessed the great proof of that claim of sovereignty in the Ascension into heaven. And so his whole view of the world and its order had been changed. Above all emperors and kings, above all armies and multitudes, he thought of the Crucified as ruling and directing the course of history, and certain in his own due time to manifest his sovereignty.

In this last clause of the opening words of salutation the Apostle had been as regardless of the technical rules of language as he had been in the first. Here also the epithets stand, not in the genitive, as in apposition with the name of Christ, but in their unimpaired majesty, in the nominative. But that salutation is hardly ended before, with the speech of one who writes as in the ecstasy of adoration, he passes from it to a doxology. And the doxology thus uttered is marked by some special characteristics. It is not, as those of St. Paul for the most part are, addressed to the Father only, or to the Father through the Son, but directly and emphatically to Jesus Christ. Knowing, as we do, the horror with which every devout Israelite shrank from ascribing Divine Glory to any but the Divine Being, we cannot but see in this the recognition that the Lord Jesus Christ, the first-begotten from the dead, was also one with the Father; that to Him, no less than to the Eternal, belonged all "glory and might" for ever and ever. If there are still those who contend that prayer and praise and adoration were not offered by the Apostolic Church to the Person of the Son, this takes its place among the foremost witnesses against their error. But the substance of the doxology is even more remarkable. The preceding words had spoken of the glory of the Christ in His own essential majesty. These tell of the special relation in which He stood to the spiritual life of the Apostle who wrote, and to all his fellow-believers: "*To him that loveth us*" (I follow the better-supported reading, which gives the present, not the past), "*and washed us*" (I see no adequate reason for preferring the reading "and freed us") "*with his own blood.*" We need scarcely dwell on the thought which had impressed itself upon the mind of the Disciple that the Lord, who had loved him with so deep and personal an affection upon earth, was still loving him, and loving others with an equal love, now that He was in heaven. There is a deeper interest in the clause which speaks of the special act of which he thought as manifesting that love. It tells us, if I mistake not, that he had entered now into the full meaning of words that had once been dark and dim to him. We can hardly suppose that the hard saying, "He that is washed needeth not save to wash his feet, but is clean every whit" (John xiii. 10), had been clear at the time to those who heard it. Who was to give them that entire cleansing? How were they to maintain their purity by that daily washing of the feet? The words came, we may believe, with a new force to the mind of the disciple who records them, when he stood by the Cross and saw the water and the blood flow from the pierced side of Him who hung there. How deep the impression of that moment was we see in the reference to it that follows immediately upon this. What we are now concerned with is the consciousness that then or afterwards it became clear within him that the Love which was consummated in that supreme act of sacrifice, the love which then seemed that of a man who "lays down his life for his friends" (John xv. 13), but was afterwards seen to be that of one who was content to die even for his foes (Rom. v. 8, 10), had a power, which nothing else could have, to kindle a new love in his own heart also; and so, through the power of that new affection, to purify him from the taint of evil and from the close-clinging impurity of his lower selfish nature. Here was "the fountain opened for sin and for uncleanness" (Zech. xiii. 1), in which the stains of the past life could be washed away. We are so familiar in hymns and sermons with the words and phrases which have flowed from this as their source, that for the most part we hardly care to trace their *genesis* and meaning; but the process of thought and feeling which I have ventured to indicate seems the only legitimate explanation of the association of ideas, at first apparently so incompatible as are those of cleansing and of blood, which we find thus brought together. The two were at any rate linked indissolubly in the mind of the Apostle. He saw in "the blood of Christ" that which "cleanseth from all sin" (1 John i. 7).

The multitude of those whom he saw in vision "arrayed in white robes" had "washed their robes and made them white in the blood of the Lamb" (Rev. vii. 13, 14).

But the train of thought thus originated led on in natural, or, more truly, perhaps, spiritual, sequence to another. Once before, as by some mystic embodiment of the great idea, or dim foreshadowing of the great fact, blood had been received as the symbol of purification. The Tabernacle and the vessels of the ministry had been sprinkled with it. In the bold language of the Epistle to the Hebrews, "almost all things are by the law purified with blood" (ix. 21). But the special cardinal instance of its use had been when Aaron and his sons had been consecrated to their priestly office. The two ideas, of being cleansed with blood and of entering on a priest's work, were accordingly closely linked together. But in that baptism of blood of which St. John thought, the washing was not limited to any priestly family, but was co-extensive with the whole company of believers. They therefore had become what the older Israel of God was at first meant to be in idea and constitution, "a kingdom of priests."[1] That

---

[1] I follow this as a better reading than that which gives "hath made us kings and priests."

sprinkling of blood upon the whole people, before the great apostasy of the golden calf, had been the symbol that they too were all consecrated and set apart for their high calling. (Exod. xix. 6, 10; xxiv. 8.) So St. John (in this instance also following in the track of the Epistle to the Hebrews) looked on the true priest's work as not limited to any order of the Church's ministry. All might offer the sacrifice of praise and thanksgiving, the incense of praise and adoration; all might pass within the veil, and enter into the Holiest and plead for themselves and for their brother in the power of the blood of Jesus. To Him, then, who had done, and was yet doing, such great things for them, the beloved Disciple offers an ascription of praise and glory and power like that which went up from the lips of every devout Israelite to the Everlasting Father.

But the thoughts of the Seer travel on to the far future. "*Behold, he cometh with clouds.*" The words that had been spoken by the Lord in his hearing in the High Priest's palace had claimed for the Christ the fulfilment of the vision of Daniel, in which the prophet had seen one like unto the Son of Man come with the clouds of heaven, even unto the Ancient of days. (Dan. vii. 13; Matt. xxvii. 14.) Even before that utterance of the truth, as he with

Peter and Andrew and James, had sat on the Mount of Olives, hearing from the Lord's lips that wondrous unveiling of the future, he had learnt that a day would come "when all the tribes of the earth shall mourn, and they shall see the Son of man coming in the clouds of heaven with power and great glory" (Matt. xxiv. 29). The reference here to that declaration is clear and unmistakable, and so far we have a proof, in a book which the latest and least traditional criticism ascribes to the reign of Nero, which, at the latest, is as early as that of Domitian, that, if not the whole Gospel of St. Matthew in its present shape, at least that prophetic discourse was already current and recognised in the Churches of Asia, or else that the memory of the writer of the Apocalypse supplied him with the selfsame record.

"*And every eye shall see him and they also which pierced him.*" Here, as elsewhere, we have words which carry us back, first, to the Gospel of St. John, and, secondly, to the teaching of an older prophet. The Fourth Gospel alone records the fact, which the writer, we must believe, alone of all the four, had seen with his own eyes, of the pierced side and of the water and the blood. (John xix. 34, 37.) The writer of this book remembers that fact, and connects it with words which are a literal Greek rendering (not, be it observed, from the version of the LXX., which translates the words quite differently) of part of Zech. xii. 10. The Gospel, the later work, as we believe, of the same writer, does explicitly what is here done implicitly, and cites the prophecy as fulfilled in the event; and with identically the same variation from the current Greek version as that which we find here. It would be difficult, I think, to find anywhere a much stronger indirect proof of identity of authorship. It is clear, however, that St. John had learnt to generalise and idealise the event to which he thus refers. As those who fell away from the faith, or became its open enemies, crucified to themselves the Son of God afresh (Heb. vi. 6), so it was not only the lance of the Roman soldier that actually pierced Him, but much more all those whose sins of act or thought, whose want of faith and love, had been to Him as those of the inhabitants of Jerusalem had been, in the language of the older prophet, cutting and *piercing* to the quick. And "*all the kindreds of the earth,*" so run the words of the Apostle, "*shall wail because of him.*" That Epiphany of the Judge in his Majesty and Righteousness cannot but call forth terror and dismay in all who under this name, "*of the earth*," earthy, are described as unholy and rebellious. The memory of past sins, the dread of penalty, the shame at having sinned against the Holiest, these will all be elements of woe and sorrow unspeakable. The words seem at first to tell not only of such an ineffable anguish, but of a wailing hopeless and irremediable. We turn, however, to the words of the older prophet, which, as we have seen, were clearly in St. John's thoughts; and there, so far from the picture of an irremediable penalty, we find that looking upon Him whom men had pierced, connected closely with the pouring out "of the spirit of grace and supplication," with a great and bitter mourning, it is true, but also with the opening even then of "the fountain for sin and for uncleanness." (Zech. xii. 10; xiii. 1.) So it was, we may believe, that the Seer, accepting the thoughts of the terror and judgment as coming from the Manifestation of One who was infinitely righteous, could contemplate that dark vision of the future without misgiving, and add, as in adoring acceptance, "*Even so, Amen.*" And then, for the first time, the form of the message changes, and the voice of the Lord is heard speaking in his own name: "*I am Alpha and Omega, the beginning and the ending*" (these latter words, however, are wanting in the best manuscripts, and are probably a gloss upon the names of the Greek letters), "*saith the Lord God*" (I follow the best manuscripts in this reading), "*which is, and which was, and is to come, the Almighty.*" I am not aware that there is any example in any writing earlier than the Apocalypse of this mystical use of the first and last letters of the Greek alphabet, and the instances which are quoted of a like employment of the corresponding letters (corresponding *i.e.* in position) of the Hebrew alphabet, א and ת, are all of much later date. So far as the evidence goes, it may well have been that St. John himself was the first to seize on that mystic significance, and to see in the two letters of the alphabet which was at least comparatively new to him, the symbol of the Eternity of God, so limitless that we can imagine nothing as either before or after it. As the words stand with the reading "*the Lord God,*" and interpreted by what has gone before in verse 4, they refer primarily to the Eternity of the Father. We need not fear lest, in adopting that reading, we should sacrifice one jot or tittle of the witness which, with the received reading, the words have been thought to bear to the divinity of the Son. The more distinctly we refer them here to "*the Almighty*" in the Old Testament sense of the word (ὁ παντοκράτωρ, the LXX. rendering of the Lord of Sabaoth — the Lord of Hosts), the more wonderful is their explicit application in the immediate sequel to Him, rather, their utterance *by* Him, who was seen in the midst of the seven golden candlesticks.

The words in which the writer of the Apocalypse describes himself, and the process by which the messages he is about to write came to him, are every way significant. "*Tribulation*" had come upon those Churches, and he was a "*fellow-sharer*" with them in the sufferings which it brought; but through the tribulation he and they were alike gaining their place "*in the kingdom.*" He repeats, *i.e.* the lesson which the Churches in that region had heard at the outset from St. Paul, that "we must through much tribulation enter into the kingdom of God" (Acts xiv. 22). But he is their partner also in the *patience* or "*endurance*," not *of* (I follow the better reading), but "*in Jesus.*" The thought expressed is not, as it is perhaps in 2 Thess. iii. 5 (if we accept our English rendering), that of "the patient waiting for Christ," nor yet of a patience like that of which Christ had been the great example, but of an endurance which had its life and energy in union with Him. He goes on to tell how it was that he found himself in Patmos. He had proclaimed the Word of God; he had borne his witness, and this was the result. It would help us but little in the work on which we have entered to picture to ourselves the rocks and shores of that island. With its scenery we have but small concern. The imagery of the visions that follow is all but entirely unaffected by the external surroundings of the Seer. At the furthest, we can but think of the deep-blue waters of the Mediterranean, now purple as wine, now green as emerald, flushing and flashing in the light like the hues on the plumage of a dove, opalescent and phosphorescent, according to the changes of sun- and moon-light, as accustoming the Apostle's eye, and, through the eye, his thoughts, to impressions of splendours and glories—the rainbow round about the throne, and the sea of crystal mingled with fire (Rev. iv. 3-6)—which we find it all but impossible to represent to the imagination, and which even he found it hard to express adequately in words.

And he was "*in the Spirit, on the Lord's day.*" I cannot hesitate for a moment to accept the current explanation of the latter phrase as meaning the first day of the week, the day of the Lord's resurrection, the day also, let us remember, of the Lord's supper. The adjective

($Κυριακός$ = belonging to the Lord), which in each case expresses the sacred character of the supper or the day, was, so far as we can trace it, either coined by St. Paul, or for the first time taken out of colloquial into written use, as applied to the former. It is found in no earlier writer. It seems probable that, fashioned as it was to express a new thought and meet a new want, it spread rapidly among the Greek-speaking Churches, and its first extension would naturally be to the day on which the disciples in each Church met together to partake of the sacred meal to which it had been originally applied.[1] Let us think, then, what that day would be to the beloved Disciple in his Patmos exile; how, absent from his flock in the body, he, at that hour of closest communion with them and with his Lord, would yet be with them in the spirit; how the very separation would throw him back more entirely upon the earlier memories of the day as that on which he had first beheld his Master as

---

[1] The same word $κυριακός$ is, according to a current, but not quite certain, etymology, the origin of Kirche, Kirk, Church, as being the Lord's house. "Cyriac," as a proper name, is another instance of its extension. Some modern philologists, however, are inclined to refer the word Church to a Gothic or Teutonic root. It is, at any rate, a suggestive fact that while the Teutonic languages of modern Europe make it the representative of "ecclesia," all the Romance languages have some word directly derived from the Greek original.

the conqueror of Hades and of Death. It was natural, if we may apply that term to the orderly sequence of spiritual phenomena, that such emotions should pass into ecstatic adoration, that the life of sense should be suspended, that he should be in the state of half-consciousness which St. Paul so well portrays: "Whether in the body or out of the body, I cannot tell: God knoweth" (2 Cor. xii.). In that trance-state so described, in which the man sees what others cannot see and hears voices which others cannot hear, and which, in this case at least, did not deprive the Seer of the power of distinctly recording afterwards what had been thus made known, the messages to the Seven Churches were revealed to him.

The first impression made on the new consciousness is that which is described as like the sound of "*a great voice, as of a trumpet.*" It woke him out of the sleep that was the transition-stage between the lower and the higher life. Its sounds thrilled through brain and nerve, as will thrill one day the trump of the archangel. He heard the words, "*I am Alpha and Omega, the first and the last,*" of which he had already reproduced the echoes. He heard too, as if in answer to unuttered and unrecorded prayers, the words which told him that there were messages from that Eternal One to each of those Churches, or communities of believers, whose wants and perils had been as a burden on his soul. If his waking thoughts had travelled, as thoughts do travel at such times and under such conditions, to those sheep of the flock of the Great Shepherd whom he had so often visited, with whom he had so often on the Lord's day broken the bread and drunk of the cup of blessing, it must have been welcome tidings to him that he could preach to them a diviner word of counsel and reproof from his place of exile than he had done when he had been living and working in the midst of them. And then he turned and looked—and the vision that met his gaze was one of glory and majesty unspeakable. The "*seven golden candlesticks*" which he there beheld would at least remind him of the seven-branched candlestick which stood in the inner sanctuary (not the Holy of Holies) of the Tabernacle and the Temple. They had borne their witness there for centuries that God was Light, and that that Light revealed itself in manifold variety growing out of a central unity.[1]

---

[1] The description of the golden candlestick in Exod. xxv., with its central stem, the three branches on either side, parting into smaller branches, with buds and flowers, and almond-like fruit on each, is singularly suggestive. It was tree-like in its form—but if so, with what meaning? Was it intended to sym-

In the vision of Zechariah—whose prophecy had, as we have seen already, been much in the mind of St. John, suggesting imagery and phraseology—it had been seen (probably after the pattern of the lamp constructed, at the time of the return from the Babylonian exile under Zerubbabel, for the restored Temple) as a "candlestick all of gold, with a bowl upon the top of it, and his seven lamps thereon, and seven pipes to the seven lamps, which are upon the top thereof" (Zech. iv. 2). To make the symbol yet more complete, and adapted to what were then the pressing necessities of the time, he saw in his vision two olive-trees feeding from their branches, through two golden pipes, the bowl through which the lamps were kept burning. He learnt in the interpretation of the symbol that the two olive-trees were the two "sons of oil," the two "anointed ones," the representatives of priestly and of civil authority, Joshua

bolise the "Tree of Life that was in the midst of the Paradise of God?" (Rev. ii. 7.) Was this the earliest expression of the Truth that in God the light and life were one, and that both flowed from Him into the spirits of his creatures? (See the present writer's *Biblical Studies*, p. 62.) I may add, as confirming this conclusion, the remarkable fact that a rough outline of the seven-branched candlestick, or lamp, occurs frequently in the Jewish cemeteries at Rome and elsewhere (Milman's *History of the Jews*, vol. iii. p. 457). Simply as such, it was not a natural ornament for a sepulchre, but if it were also the symbol of the Tree of Life, its appearance there is sufficiently accounted for.

and Zerubbabel, upon whom at that period the welfare of the nation's life depended. The candlestick, or lamp, that was thus seen in the prophet's vision was probably identical in form with that which has become familiar to us as represented on the Arch of Titus, among the spoils of Jerusalem. Here, however, we have what seems at first a modification of the symbolism, almost a new symbol. The Seer beholds not a lamp with seven branches, but seven distinct lamps. The ethical reason of the change is, perhaps, not far to seek. For him the lamp was the symbol not merely of the uncreated Light, but (so he had been taught by his Lord himself) of a Christian society, as the channel through which that light was to be diffused through the world, a lamp set upon the lamp-shaft or pedestal (Matt. v. 15). What he needed therefore was to bring out clearly the individuality of each such society, and this was done by the manner in which they were thus presented to his vision. If one were to endeavour to realise the vision as it were pictorially, it may have been that the Form which he beheld in the seven lamps stood in front of the central shaft, hiding it from view, and so leaving them to appear each in its own separate distinctness.

That Form he describes as "*like unto the*

Son of man." Taken by themselves, and standing as they do without the article, the words might be translated simply as in the great prophecy of Daniel (vii. 13), from which the title had been derived, "*One like unto a Son of man,*"[1] a form which, though arrayed in glory, was yet human. But the constant appropriation of the title by the Lord Jesus, its use by Him in the words which had stamped the expectation of His second Advent upon the minds of His disciples, forbid us to assign that lower meaning to it here. What the Seer meant his readers to understand was, that he had seen the Master whom he had known and loved.

The description that follows lies obviously beyond the region of art. It is an attempt to portray thoughts and impressions which are almost, if not altogether, beyond the reach of words. The Seer strives to represent a glory which has dazzled and confounded him. A human form, pervaded and clothed with light in all its purity, glorified and transfigured, so

---

[1] This is beyond the shadow of a doubt the right rendering in the older Revelation. Here it is, I think, open to some question. On the one hand there is no definite article in the Greek; and in our Lord's application of it to Himself the article is always found. On the other, its constant use by Him may have given to it something of the character of a proper name or title, so that, with or without the article, it could not fail to suggest a reference to Him.

that what he had once beheld on the Mount of Transfiguration seemed to pale in memory before this greater brightness, this was what he looked upon. It is important that we should remember that there had been that anticipation of the glory of the Son of man while He was yet on earth, that the Seer who now beheld the vision had then been one of "the eyewitnesses of his Majesty." It is not less important to remember how far it was now surpassed. The head and hair in their dazzling whiteness spoke at once of stainless purity and of the crown of glory of the Ancient of Days; the eyes seemed to burn into the soul with their fiery and searching gaze; the voice was like the sound of many waters; even the feet,[1] just shewn below the long robe that reached to the ankles, glowed with the same pervading bright-

---

[1] It is not, I think, important for our purpose to discuss the mysterious χαλκολίβανος — the "fine brass" of the English Version. As this is the one passage in which it is found, its meaning must be more or less conjectural. I incline with Bleek to the view that it is a hybrid compound of the Greek χαλκός and the Hebrew "*labân*"—white. Such technical words were likely enough to be current in a population like that of Ephesus, consisting largely of workers in metal, some of whom, if we may judge from the case of Alexander the coppersmith (Acts xix. 34; 2 Tim. iv. 14), were without doubt Jews. I believe the word in question to have belonged to this technical vocabulary. It is, at any rate, used by St. John as familiar and intelligible to those for whom he wrote.

ness. The other details of the manifestation are, however, more significant. The form of the Son of man is seen arrayed, not, as in the days of his ministry, in the short seamless tunic and the flowing cloak (the χίτων and ἱμάτιον, which were the common dress of the Jewish peasant), but in the long robe reaching to the feet, that had been the special garment of the High Priest. St. John uses, *i.e.* the very word ποδήρης, which stood in the LXX. version of Exod. xxviii. 31 for the *Ephod* of Aaron. And He is girded with a golden girdle, not, as of one who toils and runs, around the loins (comp. Luke xii. 35), but, as of one who had passed into the repose of sovereignty, around the breast. That the girdle should be of gold, as the symbol of that sovereignty, was almost a necessary consequence. In this combination of the received emblems of the two forms of rule there was set forth, in its simplest symbolism, that union of the kingly and the priestly offices, that revival of the priesthood after the order of Melchizedek, which the argument of the writer of the Epistle to the Hebrews had by this time made more or less familiar. And in His hand He holds seven stars (verse 16). In what way they were seen as held by Him we are not told; but the symbolism is, I venture to think, far more suggestive if we think of them as shining as precious gems would shine if used as signet-rings, than if we picture to ourselves the seven stars as held in the palm of the hand, or suspended from it as a wreath.[1] Here, at least, there is the guiding precedent of the old prophetic language. Of one king of the house of David it had been said that though he were as the "signet upon the right hand" of Jehovah, he should be plucked from it and cast away. (Jer. xxii. 24.) Of another heir to the kingly succession of that house the promise had been written, "I will take thee, O Zerubbabel, my servant, . . . saith the Lord, and will make thee as a signet" (Hagg. ii. 23). To the Eastern mind no symbol could more adequately express the preciousness of the Angels of the Churches to Him who thus held them, the honour to which He had exalted them, the care with which He watched over them.

The character of the next symbol is less ambiguous—"*Out of his mouth went a sharp*

[1] If one may venture on representing to the eye the manner in which they were thus held, I would suggest that they were seen on the inner side of the open hand, arranged in an order like that of the seven stars in the constellation of Ursa Major. It may be noticed that Philo refers both to that constellation and the Pleiades as examples of the prominence of the mystic number even in the visible and material universe.

two-edged sword." The thought expressed is obviously that of the power of the Divine Judge to discern the thoughts and intents of the heart, and to punish those which were evil and deserved punishment. The sword was thus identical with " the word of the Lord " of the older prophets (Isa. xlix. 2), and of Heb. iv. 12, " sharper than any two-edged sword, piercing even to the dividing asunder of soul and spirit, and of the joints and marrow." Here, adopting the new nomenclature of the writer, we may call it "the word of *the* WORD"—the spoken utterance of Him who Himself utters the mind and will of the Eternal Father. What the Seer beheld in vision was the expression of the truth that the message he was about to record would be conveyed in keen and piercing words, cutting through the ulcers of the soul, cutting off the diseased members, laying bare the inmost organs of the inner life, slaying those who deserved slaughter; but also wounding to heal, even slaying that He might raise as from the dead. And therefore it was that the countenance which he beheld was *" as the sun shining in his strength,"* bright and terrible to look upon, and yet the source of all life and joy. In the light of that countenance he and all men, if they walked in it, should see the light of life.

So it was in the immediate personal experience of the Disciple. As though that sword had pierced his soul, as though that light were too dazzling for mortal eye, he "*fell at his feet as dead.*" And then from that death-like trance he was roused by a touch and by a word: "*He laid his right hand upon me, saying unto me, Fear not.*" We can hardly doubt that that touch must have recalled many an hour of loving and tender companionship in what seemed now as a remote past, when he had leant his head upon the Master's breast, and had felt the hand that told of sympathy and of love laid, in hours of sorrow and perplexity, upon his shoulder, or clasping his hand in the confidence of friendship. "*Fear not!*" that too had been often heard by the disciples on the Lake of Galilee (Matt. xiv. 27; John vi. 19) in the dark hours of night. It had been the cheering watchword of his call to be one of the "fishers of men" (Luke v. 10), one of the "little flock" which the Good Shepherd had deigned to take under his especial guardianship (Luke xii. 32). Then, for the most part, it was the thought of their Lord's presence that removed their fear, the presence of One who was then "despised and rejected of men," like themselves in the outward accidents of life. That which removed the greater fear now was the assurance which the word and the touch gave him that the glorified form on which he looked was one with the Son of man, whom he had known and loved, one also with the Eternal Lord, One who had triumphed over death, the living One who had died, but was henceforth "*alive for evermore.*" The word "*Amen*" which followed, so often used by our Lord during his earthly ministry, placed this assurance of His own everlasting life, the source of all life to others, on the level of the highest truths which He had been wont to seal with this emphatic affirmation.

And to this there was added the new proclamation: "*I have the keys of death and of Hades*" (I take the words in what appears to be their true order). What thoughts would those words raise in the mind of the hearer? What abiding truths do they set forth for us? He, we know, had heard his Master speak of "the gates of Hades" (Matt. xvi. 18). He had accepted the interpretation of the old Messianic psalm, which spoke of the soul of the Christ as not having been left in Hades. He must have known the faith of St. Peter, that in his descent into Hades his Lord had, in that unseen world, preached to "the spirits in prison," who had once been disobedient (1 Pet. iii. 19), proclaiming his gospel to those that were dead, that they might be judged according to men in the flesh, but live according to God in the Spirit (1 Pet. iv. 6). He may have been familiar with the half-proverbial saying which appeared afterwards in the Targums and the Talmud, that the key of the grave was one of the four keys which the Eternal King committed to no ministering angel, but reserved exclusively in his own power and for his own use. In any case he knew, both from the language of the older prophets (Isa. xxii. 22) and from his Lord's promise to Peter (Matt. xvi. 18), that the key was the recognised symbol of supreme, though, it might be, delegated authority, of the power to open and shut, to admit and to exclude. In these words, therefore, he would hear the assurance that the shadowy realms on which men looked with terror, and which they peopled with all dark imaginings, were in very deed subject to the rule of Him who, though He had tasted death for every man, was now alive for evermore. "*Death and Hades*" —these were familiar sounds, as the names of the two great enemies of mankind, the forces that opposed the fulfilment of God's purposes and the completion of his kingdom. Now he heard that they had been despoiled of their power to harm, as afterwards he was to hear that they would deliver up the dead that were in them, and that they themselves should be cast, together with those who were not found written in the Book of Life, into "the lake of fire" (Rev. xx. 13-15). That thought was the one adequate remedy for the fear of death through which, with hardly an exception, men had been all their life-time subject to bondage (Heb ii. 15); for the secret of that fear was their want of faith that there also, in that unseen world, behind the veil, were to be traced the workings of an absolute Righteousness and an everlasting Love.

The command that followed—"*Write the things which thou hast seen, and the things which are, and the things that shall be hereafter*"—was simple and clear enough. But as yet the inner meaning of the vision that he had looked on had not been made known to him, and it was the fitting sequel to the education through which his Lord had led him while on earth, explaining to him and to his brother disciples the mysteries of the Kingdom of Heaven, which to others were veiled in parables, that here also, before he entered on the special task assigned him, he should be taught the meaning of the symbols of the seven stars that were in or on the right hand of the Son of man, and of the seven golden candlesticks in the midst of which He stood. The seven stars were, he heard, "*the angels of the seven churches.*"

The question, Who were meant by these Angels? has received very different answers. On the one hand it has been urged that everywhere else throughout the Book "angels" are angels in the ordinary acceptation of the word, superhuman messengers and ministers of God; that the term is nowhere else applied in the New Testament, nor in early Patristic writings, to any officer or teacher in the Church; that the symbolism of the visions of Daniel, in which Persia and Grecia are represented by angels (Dan. x. 20, 21; xii. i.), who are as their princes and guardians, finds a natural parallel here. On the other hand it is urged that, even admitting, what it is hard to admit, that the language of Daniel is more than symbolic, and that there are round the Eternal Throne the guardian angels of nations, with the divided counsels and conflicting interests of the peoples committed to their care, diplomatic representatives, as it were, at the court of the Great King, the words that are addressed to the angels of the Churches are altogether inapplicable except to men of like passions with ourselves. They have "laboured and not fainted," or they have to suffer "even unto death," or they have "left their first love," or they are "neither cold nor hot," and are in peril of utter rejection. I follow accordingly the majority of commentators in identifying these angels with those whom we should call the bishops of the Churches, the chief presbyters, vested with authority over other presbyters, exercising control over all the Churches of what in modern phrase would be called their diocese,—the city and its suburbs committed to their care.

But the question comes why these chief presbyters were described here, and here only, by this new title; and the answer is to be found, I believe, in the special phenomena of that transition period of the apostolic age to which we have referred the Book before us. In the earlier organisation the names of bishop and elder were, as is well known, interchangeable,[1] and the Apostles occupied a position more or less analogous to that of the bishops of later date. But at the time when St. John wrote, the personal care of St. Paul had been withdrawn from the Asiatic Churches, and had been

---

[1] It is hardly necessary to prove an admitted fact, but a reference to the following passages will shew the equivalence of the two terms: Acts xx. 17, 28; Phil. i. 1; 1 Tim. iii. 1, 8; Tit. i. 5, 7; 1 Pet. v. 1, 2.

delegated to one specially sent by him, like Timotheus, to act on his behalf in appointing, reproving, or deposing elders. What title was to be given to this new officer, this Vicar Apostolic of the primitive Church? The term "bishop" had not yet risen to the higher level in which it implied a superiority to presbyter. The name "apostle," as applied to those who had been called and chosen by Christ himself, was too high. In its other sense, as used of those who were simply the "messengers" of the Churches (2 Cor. viii. 2, 3), it was too low. The word "angels" might well commend itself at such a time as fitted to indicate the office for which the received terminology of the Church offered no adequate expression. Over and above its ordinary use it had been applied by the prophet whose writings had been brought into a new prominence by the ministry of the Baptist, to himself as a prophet (Mal. i. 1), to the priests of Israel (Mal. ii. 7), to the forerunner of the Lord (Mal. iii. 1). It had been used of those whom, in a lower sense, the Lord had sent to prepare his way before Him (Luke ix. 52), and whose work stood on the same level as that of the Seventy. Here then seemed to be that which met the want. So far as it reminded men of its higher sense it testified that the servants of God who had been called to this special office were to "lead on earth an angel's life;" that they, both in the liturgical and the ministerial aspects of their work, were to be as those who in both senses were "ministering spirits" in heaven (Heb. i. 14[1]). It helped also—and this may well have commended it—to bring the language of the Revelation into harmony with that of the great apocalyptic work of the Old Testament, the prophecy of Daniel. On the other hand, we need not wonder that it did not take a prominent place in the vocabulary of the Church. The old associations of the word were too dominant, the difficulty of distinguishing the new from the old too great, to allow of its being generally accepted. It was enough that it answered, as now, a special purpose.

That these bishop-angels of the Churches should be represented by the symbol of the stars must have seemed, as soon as the key was once given, to be simple and natural enough. They too were set in the firmament of heaven, of the kingdom of heaven, to give light upon the earth. "Their sound had gone

[1] It may be worth while to note that there are two distinct Greek words in this verse rendered by the same English word and that the first expresses the service of worship, the second the of ministration.

into all the earth" (so St. Paul had interpreted the words of the noblest of the Psalms of nature, which referred in their original meaning to the voiceless witness of the stars), "and their words unto the ends of the world" (Rom. x. 18). And for those to whom these messages were sent, the fact that they were as stars in the right hand of Christ was at once solemnising and strengthening. They were not what they were, or where they were, by chance. In the hand of Christ, subject to his power, but sustained also by his strength, safe so long as they continued there, shining in their unclouded brightness; in danger if they strayed from his protection, to be as the "wandering stars, to whom is reserved the blackness of darkness for ever" (Jude, verse 13)—this was and is a thought of comfort and of awe for all those who have been called to be successors to their office and sharers in their responsibilities.

Of the symbolism of the candlesticks, or lamps, I have already spoken. All that need be added here is that which grows out of the connection of the two symbols. The stars, shine, each in its brightness and its beauty, and if true to the light given them, will shine for ever as gems upon the right hand of the Lord of the Churches. But to give light to those that are in the house (Matt. v. 15), to diffuse the knowledge of the truth by word and yet more by act, to derive their power thus to let their light shine before men from Him who gives the oil without which the light would be extinguished — these attributes of the life of the Church were better represented by the lamps that shed their rays through the surrounding darkness. In the gloom of this world's night the light of the lamp is more serviceable to those who have to live and move and work in it than the shining of the far-off star. It is the collective action of the Christian society that makes manifest the Truth of God even more than the highest individual holiness. That the Lord was seen in the midst of the seven lamps was a witness that they too were subject to his rule and were not exempted from his care.

II.

THE EPISTLE TO EPHESUS.

THE REVELATION.

CHAPTER II.

1 UNTO the angel of the church of Ephesus write ; These things saith he that holdeth the seven stars in his right hand, who walketh in the midst of the seven golden candlesticks ;

2 I know thy works, and thy labour, and thy patience, and how thou canst not bear them which are evil : and thou hast tried them which say they are apostles, and are not, and hast found them liars :

3 And hast borne, and hast patience, and for my name's sake hast laboured, and hast not fainted.

4 Nevertheless I have *somewhat* against thee, because thou hast left thy first love.

5 Remember therefore from whence thou art fallen, and repent, and do the first works ; or else I will come unto thee quickly, and will remove thy candlestick out of his place, except thou repent.

6 But this thou hast, that thou hatest the deeds of the Nicolaitanes, which I also hate.

7 He that hath an ear, let him hear what the Spirit saith unto the churches ; To him that overcometh will I give to eat of the tree of life, which is in the midst of the paradise of God.

II.

WITH the topography of the city of Ephesus, with its history prior to the formation of a Christian Church within its walls, we are not at present concerned.[1] They have hardly the slightest appreciable bearing upon the interpretation of the words which now come before us. All that we need to remember is that its far-famed Temple of Artemis —visited by pilgrims from all quarters of the Empire, who carried away with them on their departure the silver shrines made by Demetrius and his craftsmen as memorials of their visit; surrounded by a population of priests, guides, artisans, who by that craft had their living— made it one of the great centres of Heathenism; and that when St. Paul and his companions,

[1] I may, perhaps, be permitted to refer the reader who wishes for information on these points to a small book—one of a series on "St. Paul's Work in the great Heathen Centres"—on Tarsus, Antioch, and Ephesus, published by the Society for Promoting Christian Knowledge.

following in the footsteps of Apollos, planted the Church of Christ there, they must have felt that they were gaining a victory over one of the strongholds of the powers of darkness. Its religion was, however, very largely Oriental rather than Hellenic in its character. The image of the many-breasted Artemis who was there worshipped, which was fabled to have fallen from heaven, looking to our eyes like an Indian idol, would have offended the cultivated taste of an Athenian, accustomed to gaze on the works of Phidias and Praxiteles. As in all Eastern cities, its people dealt much in magic and charms and incantations, and the Ephesian talismans, or "books of curious arts" (the γράμματα Ἐφέσια of Greek writers), had a world-wide renown, and fetched an almost fabulous price (Acts xix. 19). There, as in most commercial cities, Jews had found their way in large numbers, and had their synagogues open to proselytes and inquirers. Not a few of them drifted more or less openly into connection with the superstitions against which they ought to have borne their witness. They were coppersmiths, like Alexander (2 Tim. iv. 14), and had apparently trade relations with the workmen of Demetrius (Acts xix. 38). They boasted of their powers in the cases commonly ascribed to demoniacal possession, and, like the seven sons of Sceva, who claimed to be in some sense a chief priest of the house of Aaron, sought gain and fame as exorcists (Acts xix. 13-16). In spite of this decline from their true dignity, perhaps in proportion to it, they were conspicuous for their fanatic zeal for holy places and for holy customs, and were the first to raise their outcry against St. Paul when, as they thought, he had taken an uncircumcised Ephesian within the precincts of the temple, beyond the wall of partition, which it was death for any Gentile to pass (Acts xxi. 27, 21).

The stages of progress in the Christian community at Ephesus may be traced with sufficient distinctness. First, there had been the preaching of some disciples of the Baptist, reviving the zeal of the Jews, calling them to repentance, imposing more rigid rules of life (Acts xix. 3). Then had come Apollos himself, as yet knowing only the baptism of John, but with wider thoughts, and teaching more fully than they had done the "first principles of the oracles of God" (Heb. v. 12). Then had come Aquila and Priscilla, with their more perfect knowledge, teaching the way of the Lord as St. Paul taught it, though, we must believe, with less power and completeness (Acts xviii. 24).

Then St. Paul himself appeared, preaching his gospel, at first in the synagogues to his own people of the stock of Abraham, afterwards to the disciples and to Gentile inquirers as a separate body in the lecture-room (belonging, possibly, to a school of medicine) that was known as the property of Tyrannus.¹ Wonders of a kind precisely adapted to meet the faith of the Ephesians in charms and talismans were wrought by his hands, and even by the handkerchiefs and aprons to which contact with his flesh had imparted a mysterious power (Acts xix. 9-12). The result of this two-fold influence was the rapid conversion of a large number of the Heathen, chiefly among those who had been practitioners in the arts of sorcery. They brought the books in which they had learnt to see the work of the enemy of God, and burnt them publicly in some open square or market-place (Acts xix. 19). How full and thorough was the success of the Apostle in his

---

¹ The name Tyrannus occurs in the "Columbarium" of Livia as belonging to a physician of the Imperial household. Such occupations often descended, with the name, from father to son among the freedmen attached to the Imperial household; and I venture to surmise that this Tyrannus also was of the same calling, that the "beloved physician" who was St. Paul's friend and fellow-worker may have been acquainted with him, and that it was through his influence that the use of the lecture-room was obtained.

mission-work among his new disciples, how rapid the progress which they made in Christian thought and feeling, we find from his earnest desire to see the elders of the Ephesian Church on his last journey to Jerusalem, even though he could not personally visit their city, and from the words of parting counsel which he addressed to them. He who spake to others as to carnal, as to babes in Christ, had not shunned to preach to them " all the counsel of God" (Acts xx. 27). In the midst of constant opposition, with the fear of frequent plots, amid tears and trials, he had done his work. But even then his eye saw signs of evils as yet half latent: "the grievous wolves not sparing the flock," Jewish persecutors from without, the "men from among their ownselves speaking perverse things," who should draw away disciples after them—these filled him with anxious and sad forebodings. And so they parted, as they both then thought, never to meet again (Acts xx. 17-38).

So far as we can gather from the Epistle to the Ephesians, no tidings had reached the Apostle in the interval to cause him fresh anxiety. Its tone is throughout free from the indignation or warning or reproof which we find in so many of his letters. He remembers his intercourse with them with thankfulness and joy. He has heard of their faith in the Lord Jesus and their love towards all saints. He appeals to them as able to understand his knowledge in the mystery of Christ. No messenger has come from them, as Epaphras had come from Colossæ, to tell him that false teachers had crept in and were subverting the gospel which he had preached. He must have looked forward to his return to them—and we know from the letter to Philemon (verse 22) that he was looking forward — with joy and hope. The Pastoral Epistles, if we accept them as St. Paul's, and place them in their right relation to his life, shew us how bitterly he was disappointed. False teachers had come, claiming the authority of Rabbis, desirous to be teachers of the Law, and yet ignorant of its true scope and office (1 Tim. i. 7). There were perverse disputings of men of corrupt minds, having a form of godliness, but denying its power; creeping into houses and leading captive silly women laden with sins (2 Tim. iii. 4-7). His own followers and friends had not the courage to stand by him, and all men forsook him (2 Tim. i. 15). It was necessary to leave Timotheus behind him to maintain purity of doctrine and completeness of organisation. And even he, zealous and devoted as he was, seemed hardly equal to the burden that was thus laid upon him. He was too young to speak with the authority of a wide experience, younger than many of those whom he was called to control and to reprove. He was weak in health, and the overstrained asceticism which he had imposed on himself as a rule of life tended to want of promptness and of energy (1 Tim. v. 23). He needed, even in the last parting words of counsel which St. Paul ever wrote to him, to be stirred to fresh activity, to be warned against the spirit of timidity that shrinks from hardship and from conflict, against the profane and vain babblings which, under the show of a mystical elevation that seemed to men as a rising from the death of sin, were denying that there was any other resurrection (2 Tim. i. 6, 7).

It was necessary to bring before our thoughts what we know of the Ephesian Church just as the great Apostle of the Gentiles was about to pass from the scene of his labours, that so we might the better enter into the spirit of the message sent to it through the pen of the beloved Disciple. The shorter the interval between the two —and, on the assumption which I have adopted as to the date of the Apocalypse, the interval must have been very short—the closer must have been the resemblance between the state of things described in the Pastoral Epistles and that pre-supposed in the message with which we are now dealing. But the facts lead us, if I mistake not, to a conclusion of deeper and more personal interest. Timotheus had been left in charge of that Church. That was the flock committed to him as one of the chief shepherds. If we think of the Angel of the Church of Ephesus as its personal ruler and representative, there is at least a strong presumption in favour of our thinking of the words before us as addressed to none other than to St. Paul's true son in the faith. It will be seen that a closer examination of the message confirms this conclusion.

It is noteworthy that each one of the messages opens with a description of Him who speaks them, embodying one or more of the characteristic attributes given in the preceding chapter. It is, perhaps, impossible to connect in each case the attribute thus selected with the wants or trials of each particular Church; but there can be little doubt that as Ephesus stands first in order of importance among the Seven Churches, and so the fact that He who sends the message "*holdeth the seven stars in his right hand*" and "*walketh in the midst of the seven golden candlesticks,"* is that on which most stress is laid. He holds the stars as one who rejoices in their brightness so long as they shine clearly, who sustains, protects, and guides them as He guides the stars of heaven in their courses, who can and will cast them away, even though they were as the signet on His right hand, should they cease to shine. He walks among the candlesticks as One who knows and judges all that makes the lamps burn brightly or dimly, who feeds the lamp with the oil of His grace, and trims it with the discipline of His love that it may burn more brightly, and who, if it cease to burn, though He will not quench the smoking flax while as yet there is a hope of revival, will yet remove the lamp out of its place, and give to another that work of giving light to those that are in His spiritual house, which it has failed to accomplish.

If I am right in my inference from the assumed early date of the Apocalypse, the words that follow ought to present some striking points of coincidence with the language addressed to Timothy in the Pastoral Epistles; and this, if I mistake not, they do in a measure which leaves hardly the shadow of a doubt. The work, the labour, the endurance—these are precisely what St. Paul acknowledges in his true son in the faith, and exhorts him to abound in them more and more. He reminds him that the husbandman that *laboureth* must be the first partaker of the fruits (2 Tim. ii. 6); calls on him to be "a *workman* that needeth not to be ashamed" (2 Tim. ii. 15); to do "the *work* of an evangelist," and to "*endure* afflictions" (2 Tim. iv. 5). Still more definitely do we find in the words of praise that follow that which corresponds to the Apostle's counsels. With reiterated earnestness we find him warning his true son in the faith against false teachers, such as Hymenæus, Alexander, Philetus; against those who gave heed to seducing spirits and doctrines of demons; against profane and vain babblings, whether they came from Judaizing teachers on the one hand or the fantastic dreams of Greek or Gnostic speculation on the other. One who had acted on these cautions might well have earned the commendation bestowed on the Angel of the Church of Ephesus: "*Thou canst not bear them that are evil, and thou hast tried them which say that they are apostles and are not, but hast found them liars.*" To hate evil, to feel the presence of those who are persistent in it as an intolerable burden, to try the claims of those who used great names to cloke it, by some certain test, like that which St. Paul (1 Cor. xii. 3) and St. John himself, here also agreeing with his brother apostle, had elsewhere suggested (1 John iv. 2, 3), by their agreement with the truth on which the faith of the Church rested, that Christ Jesus had come in the flesh; this was no small work to have done, no light praise to have deserved.

The question who these teachers were, who said they were apostles and were not, is not one which can be answered with any certainty. Doubtless the leaders of every sect and heresy at the opposite poles of error were in the habit of putting forth such claims. The balance of probability inclines, I think, in favour of the view that they were *not* identical with those who are afterwards named as Nicolaitanes, and that they represent the leaders of the Judaizing anti-Pauline party in the Asiatic Churches. These, we know, claimed to be apostles, either of Christ himself or of the Church at Jerusalem, with special and extraordinary powers, the "very chiefest *apostles*" of 2 Cor. xii. 11. Of these St. Paul speaks as "false *apostles*, deceitful workers," doing the work of Satan, and yet disguised as angels of light (2 Cor. xi. 13, 14). Those who followed him with ceaseless hostility in Galatia, Corinth, Philippi, and Colossæ were hardly likely to leave Ephesus untouched; and it is noticeable that among the errors against which his warning is most earnest in the Pastoral Epistles, those which are Jewish and legal occupy the foremost place (1 Tim. i. 7; Tit. i. 14). Those who do not come to the study of the Apocalypse with a preconceived theory that it is an anti-Pauline polemic, will find a confirmation of this view in the corresponding words in the message to the Church of Smyrna against those "who say that they are Jews, and are not, but are of the synagogue of Satan" (Rev. ii. 9).

The words that follow, though they seem for the most part to repeat the praise already given, present some special points of interest. Then the Angel of the Church had been praised because he could not *bear* the evil workers. Now he is commended because he has *borne* so much. To be intolerant of evil, and to be tolerant of all besides, to *bear* the burdens of other men (Gal. vi. 2), their weaknesses, or coldness, or inattention, to *bear* also the burden and heat of the day,—all this belongs to the true pastor. In this way he *bears* the cross which his Lord bore before him. And with this there is the renewed mention of "endurance," not simply the passive resignation to suffering which we commonly associate with the word "patience," but the temper of calm heroic stedfastness which belongs to him "who endureth to the end," and therefore wins his ultimate and complete deliverance from evil. And this endurance has been for the name of Christ, and has shewn itself in many labours (note the use of the self-same word as in 1 Tim. v. 17; 2 Tim. ii. 6) which have not, arduous as they were, led to weariness or sloth.[1]

It was significant, as a token of the gentleness and tenderness of the Judge, that all that was good should be fully acknowledged first, and that not till then should the evil that threatened its completeness be noticed with words of warning. *That*, we may note, is ever the true method of those who enter in any measure into the mind of Christ. Every Epistle of St. Paul (with, perhaps, the solitary exception of that to the Galatians, where the

---

[1] The various readings require a word of notice. The greater uncial Manuscripts give ουκ ἐκοπίασας, or οὐ κεκοπίακας. "Thou hast not toiled," and nothing more. The seeming difficulty of this use of the verb, as a word of praise, led (1) to the omission of the negative, and then (2) to the insertion of "thou hast not fainted," by way of expressing the original thought more clearly. Taking the above reading we must understand it as if it were, "Thou hast not toiled wearily," *i e.* "hast not felt thy labour to be a toil."

need was urgent and the peril great) is a practical illustration of it. The thought that He with whom we have to do as at once Judge and Friend and Advocate, judges us after this manner, not closing His eyes to any evil that He discerns in us, but also not extreme to mark what is done amiss, and recognising the good He has enabled us to do even more fully than we ourselves can recognise it, is one which may well come to the minister of Christ in times when his spirit droops within him and he has misgivings as to his labours and their result, with a power to strengthen and ennoble.

The special nature of the fault reproved is, I believe, entirely in accordance with the view which I have taken as to the person who was thus addressed. No one can read the Epistles to Timothy without feeling that, in the midst of all St. Paul's love for his disciple, his recognition of his loyalty, purity, earnestness, there is a latent tone of anxiety. The nature with which he had to do was emotional even to tears (2 Tim. i. 4), ascetic (1 Tim. v. 23), devout (2 Tim. i. 5); but there was in it a tendency to lack of energy and sustained enthusiasm. To supply this defect he exhorts him once and again to be strong, and to endure hardness; to stir up, *i.e.* to rekindle (ἀναζωπυρεῖν, 2 Tim.

i. 6), the grace of God; to continue in the things he had learnt, knowing of whom he had learnt them (2 Tim. iii. 14). Such an one falls easily into labours that are genuine as far as they go, and yet are not pervaded by the fervour and energy of love. Whether the "first love" is that which has God, or Christ, or man for its object, I am not careful to inquire; for the true temper of love or charity includes all three; but it is more important to insist that the defect spoken of was one which attached to the angel or bishop of the Church personally, and only to the Church at large so far as it was represented by him and influenced by his example. The "first love" which had been "left" was accordingly not that of the bride for the bridegroom of her espousal, as in Jeremiah ii. 2, but rather that of the friend of the bridegroom, loving and unselfish, whose work it was, the work which St. Paul had claimed as his own in writing to the Corinthians, to bring the bride to her betrothed and, with loving care, to guard her from defilement (2 Cor. xi. 2, 3).

It has been urged, on the assumption that the words point only or chiefly to the shortcomings of the Church of Ephesus as distinct from its ruler, that they supply an almost decisive proof of the theory which assigns the

Apocalypse to the time of Domitian.[1] The change, it is said, is too great, the falling away from the first love too complete, to have taken place in any shorter interval. I cannot but think (1) that the personal reference for which I have contended is open to no such objection; and (2) that, even on the assumption of there being a reference, direct or indirect, to the condition of the Ephesian Church, those who lay stress on this objection have dwelt too much on the bright side of the picture presented in the Epistle to the Ephesians, and too little on those darker features which, as we have seen, were already coming into prominence before the ministry of St. Paul had reached its close. What we meet with here is certainly not otherwise than consistent with the warnings and the fears, the all but total desertion, and the thickening heresies which the Pastoral Epistles bring before us. If anything, it indicates something even of a revival, partial though not complete, from the state there portrayed; and we may legitimately connect that revival, both as regards the Church and its representative, with the parting counsels of the Apostle.

The warnings and the counsels which follow

[1] Archbishop Trench, "Seven Churches," p. 73.

on this reproof have a deep ethical significance. "*Remember, therefore, from whence thou art fallen; and repent, and do the first works.*" The words bring before our thoughts one of the functions of the awful gifts of memory in the spiritual education of the individual soul. As it is true,—

> "That a sorrow's crown of sorrow is remembering happier things,"

so also is it true that the first step towards repentance is to call to mind, distinctly and vividly, the highest moments that we have known in our religious experience. There may come a time when that will be the sharpest pang of a sorrow almost or altogether hopeless, when the recollection that we have been illumined, and tasted of the heavenly gift and the powers of the world to come (Heb. vi. 4, 5), will but make us feel more bitterly the difficulty or impossibility of renewal. But, short of that, the memory of the past, however painful, is yet remedial. It tells us of the blessedness of which we have once been capable, which we have actually attained, and therefore may attain again, and so far is an element of encouragement as well as sorrow—of repentance and not of mere remorse. We can yet look back upon the height which we once had reached, and slowly and with painful steps begin to climb again. Out of that memory springs a true contrition and a stedfast effort. And the counsel which follows is precisely that which meets the exigencies of the case. It may not be possible to renew at once the *"first love."* The old fervour and enthusiasm of faith will not come back at our bidding or our wish. We must take that which, so long as we retain our power to choose, does lie within our reach, and do the *"first works"* — in this case those very works on which the Lord of the Churches had already bestowed his praise; and then, in due time, the warmth will come back to the heart which, in spite even of its own coldness, has persevered in duty. It is possible, though there is no virtue without faith, to gain faith by virtue. It is possible, in like manner, to regain the first love by doing the first works.

The call to repentance is followed by a warning, — "*Or else I will come unto thee quickly, and will remove thy candlestick out of its place, except thou repent.*" The words shew that the "coming of the Lord" had gained a wider and, in some sense, deeper meaning than that which we commonly attach to the second advent. That to which the warning points is not the great far-off event fixed in the everlasting counsels, but the Judgment-day of the language of the Old Testament, the "day of the Lord," whose coming may be averted or delayed by repentance, hastened by impenitence and defiance. Such days of the Lord come, in the course of the world's history, on all nations and churches that are faithless to their trust. The judgment lingers, the wheels of the Lord's chariot tarry, and men eat and drink, plant and build, marry and are given in marriage, as though all things would go on as they are for ever, and then He "*comes quickly*," in one or other of the sore judgments which are sent as the chastisment of their want of faith and their evil deeds. Here the judgment threatened was determined by the symbolism of the vision. The lamp was not burning brightly. If it were rekindled and trimmed and fed with oil, well. If not, there would come on it the sentence which falls on all unfaithfulness, and the lamp should be removed. The Church which had not let its light shine before men would lose even its outward form and polity, and be as though it had never been.

The Church and its ruler are here, in some measure at least, identified. Unless he repents and does the first works, the society over which he rules, and which is represented by him, will suffer the penalty which attaches to the failure of faith and love in which it has been a sharer. So it is always in the history of nations and of churches. But it would, I believe, be an error to think of the warning and the exhortations as addressed simply to the Church as such, and not to the angel or ruler individually. Much rather is it true that this is urged upon his conscience as a motive to lead him to repentance, that his sins, even though they are negative rather than positive in their character, tend to bring about that terrible result. One whose heart was in his work, who had learnt to look on the Church committed to him with a deep and anxious tenderness, would feel that to be a greater penalty than any personal chastisement. To have the blood of souls that perished required at his hand, to see his work destroyed, even though he himself should be saved, so as by fire, to lose that to which he had looked forward as his joy and crown of rejoicing,— this was and is the penalty of the shepherd who is even partially unfaithful, who has "*left his first love.*" For those who fill high places to see systems collapsing, an organisation disorganised, polity giving way to anarchy; for those who have a lower work to perceive that they are not gaining, but losing, ground, that worshippers are scattered and listeners few, and that their own want of love infects their people —this is the penalty, as by an inevitable law, of their transgression. That over which they have not watched is " decaying and waxing old." The next stage of " vanishing away," the removal of the candlestick, is not far distant.

I am not disposed to dwell, as most commentators have done, on the present desolate condition of the town of *Agio-solouk*, which represents by a few scattered huts what was once the Ephesus of world-wide fame, as shewing that the warning was neglected and that the penalty at last came. Doubtless that condition illustrates the working of the law which was proclaimed in the message as a prophecy, in the higher sense of that word ; but the time which elapsed before the decay and ruin were brought about carries us too far beyond the horizon indicated by that " coming quickly " for us to look upon it as the distinct fulfilment of a prediction. Rather may we see such a fulfilment under its brighter aspects in the fact that when we next come across traces of the spiritual condition of the Church of Ephesus it is to recognise a marked change for the better, a revival of the old energy of life and love. When Ignatius addressed his Epistle to that

Church, about half a century after what we have assumed as the date of the Apocalypse, he found it under the care of an Onesimus (whether the runaway slave of Colossæ or another of the same name, we cannot say), and abounding in spiritual excellences. It gives proof of a fulfilment of prophecy of another kind than that commonly dwelt on to find that the message had done its work. The points on which the Martyr touches are in singular harmony with the counsel given in the message now before us. That in which he rejoiced was that the believers at Ephesus and their bishop " had *rekindled* their life" (ἀναζωπυρήσαντες, the selfsame word as in 2 Tim. i. 6) "in the blood of God,"—that no sect or heresy was found among them. They "had not suffered those who came bringing an evil doctrine to sow their tares among the wheat, but had closed their ears against them." They carried God and Christ in their hearts, and so became as temples; they were *Theophori, Christophori, Naophori*. And so the sentence was at least deferred, and for many a long year the candlestick was not removed, and the Church of Ephesus, which had thus been warned, took its place in the history of the Church Catholic as bearing its witness, in the third Œcumenical Council

(A.D. 431), to the great central truth on which St. Paul and Ignatius (*ad Ephes.* c. 9), had alike laid stress, that "God was manifested in the flesh."

And then once more, and as pointing to that which was a gleam of hope even amidst the symptoms of decay that had called for the word of warning, there came words of recognition and of praise. "*This thou hast, that thou hatest the deeds of the Nicolaitanes, which I also hate.*" The questions who these Nicolaitanes were, whence they took their name, what were their hateful deeds, are, I need scarcely say, among the vexed problems of the history of the apostolic age, for the solution of which we have no satisfying data. On the one side there is the Patristic, but by no means primitive, tradition that the Proselyte of Antioch, whose name appears in the list of the Seven in Acts vi. 5, had either himself fallen away from the faith, or had by unguarded words given occasion of offence to those that followed him ; that he had taught men to abuse ($\pi\alpha\rho\alpha\chi\rho\hat{\eta}\sigma\theta\alpha\iota$) the flesh in the sense of punishing and afflicting it, and that men had taken the word as meaning that they might use it to the full, and conquer their appetites by indulging them till they ceased to stimulate, and that thus, in order to shew that lust had no power over them, they lived in what the conscience of true Christians condemned as hateful impurities.[1] On the other we have the conjectures of modern critics that the very word was a play upon the name so prominent about this time both in these very messages and in other apostolic writings—the name of Balaam the son of Beor, after whom many had gone astray (2 Pet. ii. 15), and had run greedily (Jude, verse 11), who had taught Balak to cast a stumbling-block before the children of Israel, to eat things sacrificed unto idols and to commit fornication.[2] The mention of the two as distinct, though cognate in their corruptions and impurities, in the message to the Church of Pergamos (Rev. ii. 14, 15) seems decisive against absolute identification; and I incline, with some doubt, to the

---

[1] See the articles on "Nicolaos" and the "Nicolaitanes," in Smith's *Dictionary of the Bible*. The earliest writer who states that the sect so-called claimed Nicolaos the Proselyte as their founder is Irenæus. Clement of Alexandria accepts the story that his teaching had been perverted in the manner above described. Epiphanius imputes the corrupt practices of the sect to the actual example and direct teaching of their founder.

[2] Nicolaos ("conqueror of the people") is identified with Balaam, according to one etymology of the latter word, as the "lord," according to another as the "devourer," of the people. Both derivations are, however, uncertain, and the best Hebraists (Gesenius and Fürst, the latter admitting the possibility of "devourer") explain the name as meaning, "not of the people," *i.e.*, an alien and foreigner.

old Patristic view that the sect so described took its name, under some colourable plea, from Nicolaos the Proselyte, and reserve what has to be said as to the error of Balaam till we come to it in its own place. It is enough for the present to note the fact that any feeling of righteous hatred of evil, of loathing for that which corrupts and defiles, is welcomed by the Lord of the Churches as a sign of life. As long as there is the capacity for this indignation there is hope. When this also fails, and men tolerate and accept impurity of words and acts,—when conscience is seared, as with a red-hot iron, then the last sign of life has passed away and decay and putrescence have set in.

Lastly, we have the promise of reward with which this, like all the other messages, ends. Attention is called to it in the self-same words that our Lord had so often used, almost, it might be said, as a formula of teaching, in his earthly ministry: "Whoso hath ears to hear, let him hear" (Matt. xi 15; xiii. 9); "*He that hath an ear let him hear what the Spirit saith unto the churches.*" And the promise in this case carries us back, as so much of the recorded teaching of St. John does elsewhere, to the earliest records of the Bible,[1]—to the opening

---

[1] See a Paper on "The Book of Genesis and the Revelation of St. John," in the *Bible Educator*, vol. i. p. 27.

chapters of the Book of Genesis. "*To him that overcometh will I give to eat of the tree of life, which is in the midst of the paradise of God.*"

We remember, as we read the words, that the Apostle had once before heard that promise of "paradise" from the lips of his Lord; so far as His recorded teaching goes, once, and once only (Luke xxiii. 43). Both in the general absence of the word and in that solitary use of it we may reverently recognise a profound wisdom, adapting the phases under which it presented the truth to the capacities and necessities of those who were to be recipients of it. In the popular speech of Judaism, in the legends alike of Pharisees and the multitude the word "paradise" (as now among the followers of Mahomet) brought with it the imagery of sensuous enjoyment—of a region of fair trees and pleasant fruits and clear streams, and the soft south-west blowing for evermore. He, the Teacher, was leading His disciples to a more spiritual idea of the blessedness of the life to come—say, rather, of the life eternal—and therefore brought it before them under the aspect of a kingdom in which the supreme blessedness was to gaze upon the face of the King and to be made glad with the joy of His countenance. But that thought of a kingdom required in its turn a preparatory training; without some such teaching as that of the Sermon on the Mount it was likely to suggest such a restored monarchy, having its seat at Jerusalem, as that of which Jewish zealots had dreamt and were yet dreaming; and, therefore, to that poor sufferer on the cross—the wild outlaw, whose one element of religious life had, we may believe, been the hope, in childish years long past, of a garden of delight in which he should wander at his will—He spake the word which gave comfort and hope, "This day thou shalt be with me in paradise."

And now the beloved Disciple hears once more the same word from the lips of the same Lord, in the highest moment of spiritual consciousness, as part of the apocalypse of eternal truths. So it is that extremes meet—that the language of symbols meet the necessities of children and child-like souls, ceases often to attract or to edify those who are in an intermediate state of growth, and then, when the understanding is ripened and mere abstract ideas have done their work of formulating and defining, is found to be, after all, their best, if not their only adequate exponent. The Christian of highest culture and most enlarged experience falls back upon the imagery of the Golden City and the Delectable Mountains, and the Paradise of God and the Tree of Life.

The revival of this last symbol in the pages of the Apocalypse is in many ways suggestive. Prominent as it had been in the primæval history, it had remained unnoticed in the teaching where we should most have looked for its presence,—in that of the Psalmists and the Prophets of the Old Testament. Only in the Proverbs of Solomon had it been used in a sense half-allegorical, half-mystical. Wisdom was a "tree of life" to them that laid hold on her (Prov. iii. 18); and the same glorious predicate was affirmed of the fulfilment of the heart's desire (Prov. xiii. 12); of the fruit of the righteous (Prov. xi. 30); of the wholesome and health-giving tongue (Prov. xv. 4). In connection with the revival of the symbol in the Apocalypse it may be noted (1) that it was the natural sequel of the fresh prominence that had recently been given, as we have seen, to the thought of Paradise; and (2) that the writings of Philo had specifically called attention to the Tree of Life as being the mystical type of the highest form of wisdom and of holiness—the fear of God ($\theta\epsilon o\sigma\epsilon\beta\epsilon\iota a$), by which the soul attains to immortality. We trace in other things at least the indirect influence of Philo's teaching on the thoughts and language of St. John; and as we must assume that all imagery is adapted, even in the words of the Divine Speaker, to the minds of those who hear, there seems no reason why we should not admit the working of that influence here.

It may be asked, however, What is the meaning of the symbol as thus used,—how are we to translate it into the language of more abstract truth? And here, if I mistake not, the more developed form of the symbol at the close of the Apocalypse gives us the true answer: "The tree of life bare twelve manner of fruits, and yielded her fruit every month, and the leaves of the tree were for the healing of the nations" (Rev. xxii. 2). The leaves and the fruit obviously represent, the one the full and direct, the other the partial and indirect, workings of that eternal life which St. John thought of as manifested in the Incarnate Word. The "healing of the nations," the elevation of their standard of purity and holiness, of duty and of love,—this has been the work of that partial knowledge which the Church of Christ has been instrumental in diffusing. Its influence has counteracted the deadly working of the fruit of the other tree of "the knowledge of good and evil," which we trace as due to a wisdom that is earthly, sensual, devilish. But to "*eat of the fruit of the tree*" implies a more complete fruition, a higher communion and fellowship with the source of life. And here, therefore, I cannot but think that the promise of the Judge points to the truth that He is Himself, now as ever, the "exceeding great reward" (Gen. xv. 1) of those that serve Him faithfully, that the symbol veils the truth that "this is life eternal, to know the only true God and Jesus Christ whom He has sent" (John xvii. 3).

And that reward is promised "*to him that overcometh.*" If anything were wanted to complete the evidence of a resemblance in thought and phrase in all the writings ascribed to the authorship of St. John, it would be found in the prominence of this word in all of them. Here it is the burden of every message. "I have *overcome* the world"—this was the assurance given to the disciples by their Master immediately before that prayer which, as the great High Priest of mankind, He offered up for them and all His people (John xvi. 33). The self-same word is echoed in the Epistles. To *overcome* the wicked one is the glory of the young men who are faithful to their calling

(1 John ii. 13, 14),—"that which is born of God *overcometh* the world" (1 John v. 4). "This is the victory that *overcometh* the world, even our faith," the faith of him that believeth that Jesus is the Son of God (1 John v. 4, 5). In the other Gospels it occurs but once, and then with but little emphasis (Luke xi. 22). In the Epistles of St. Paul it meets us once only, and then in the simply ethical precept, "Be not overcome of evil, but overcome evil with good" (Rom. xii. 21). It was reserved for St. John[1] at once to record, to echo, and to develop throughout his writings the words which he had heard from his Master's lips; and through him they have become part of the inheritance of Christendom, and have carried, and will carry to the end of time, strength and comfort to every faithful soldier in that great warfare against evil in which Christ is the Captain of our salvation.

[1] The verb occurs, it may be noted, twenty times in the writings of St. John.

III.

THE EPISTLE TO SMYRNA.

THE REVELATION.

CHAPTER II.

8 AND unto the angel of the church in Smyrna write; These things saith the first and the last, which was dead, and is alive;

9 I know thy works, and tribulation, and poverty, (but thou art rich) and I *know* the blasphemy of them which say they are Jews, and are not, but *are* the synagogue of Satan.

10 Fear none of those things which thou shalt suffer: behold, the devil shall cast *some* of you into prison that ye may be tried; and ye shall have tribulation ten days: be thou faithful unto death, and I will give thee a crown of life.

11 He that hath an ear, let him hear what the Spirit saith unto the churches; He that overcometh shall not be hurt of the second death.

III.

THE messages that follow that to the Church of Ephesus stand in one respect in very striking contrast to it. There we are able, through the Acts of the Apostles and the Epistles of St. Paul, to follow the history of the Christian community from its very birth; to trace the influences that had acted on it; to see in what way the picture brought before us in the Apocalypse was the result of those influences. Here we know nothing of the previous history. But for this mention of the Churches we should not have known that any Christian congregations had been planted there. Knowing that they were so planted we can at best conjecture that they owed their origin to the evangelising activity of St. Paul, or his associates in the mission-work of the Church, during his residence at Ephesus, and that they had become personally known to St. John when he succeeded to the care of the Asiatic Churches.

Nor does it help us here, any more than in the case of Ephesus, to fall back upon the pre-Christian history of Smyrna as a city. That it had been wealthy, populous, commercial, from the remote period that had preceded the Persian conquest; that it claimed, with other cities (six or seven), to have been the birthplace of Homer; that, after suffering great injury from an earthquake in the early part of the reign of Tiberius, it had risen from its ruins into fresh magnificence; that it courted and gained the favour of that Emperor and his successors,—all this is, for our present purpose, of little moment. It is, perhaps, something more to the point to remember that it was as famous for the worship of Dionysos as Ephesus was for that of Artemis, and that the mysteries and games which were held yearly in his honour were a prominent feature in its life. It followed, almost as a matter of course, from its wealth and trade, that it would attract a considerable population of Jews, and that these would occupy there much the same position as at Ephesus,[1] worshipping in their synagogues, zealous for their faith, some of them welcoming

---

[1] The prominence of the Jews in the history of the martyrdom of Polycarp at a later date shews how numerous they then were. (*Mart. Polyc.* c. 12, 13, 17.)

the new doctrine of the preachers of the Cross as the completion of that faith, some of them hating and reviling it even more than they hated the Heathenism by which they were surrounded. In such a city it was natural that the believers in the name of Christ should suffer persecution. It is clear that they had not escaped the storm which swept over the Asiatic Churches at the time of St. Paul's last visit, and which had apparently burst out with fresh violence at the time when the beloved Disciple was suffering for the faith in his exile in Patmos. Possibly its comparative remoteness from the great centre of apostolic activity at Ephesus exposed it more to the excitement of fear and agitation which persecution inevitably brings with it.

To the Angel of that Church accordingly the Lord, who speaks the word in season to them that are weary (Isa. l. 4), reveals Himself by a name that speaks of permanence and calm, of victory over all disturbing forces, victory all the more complete and wonderful because it came after apparent failure—"*These things saith the First and the Last, which was dead and is alive.*" Those who were struggling, suffering, dying for the faith, were the servants of no party-leader, no founder of a sect, no prophet with a temporary mission, but of One to whom all the æons of the world's history, all wars and revolutions and the rise and fall of kingdoms were but as "moments in the eternal silence." They might be tempted to think their cause desperate; they might seem to be fighting against overwhelming odds; death in all the myriad forms which the subtle cruelty of persecution could devise might appear imminent, but He who "*was dead and is alive*" could give them there also a victory like his own.[1]

Nor were the words that followed less distinctive in their consoling power: He knew their "*works*," their "*tribulation*," and their "*poverty*." The last word is specially suggestive as pointing to that which weighed most oppressively on the minds of the suffering community of Smyrna. Persecution has its heroic and exciting side, and under its stimulus men do and dare much; but when, in addition to this, there is the daily pressure of ignoble

---

[1] I can hardly bring myself to accept Dean Blakesley's suggestion (*Dictionary of the Bible*, art. "Smyrna"), that the words imply a reference to the mythical legend of the death and reviviscence of Dionysos, which, at Smyrna as elswhere, was prominent in the mysteries that bore his name. That legend must surely have been altogether foreign to the thoughts of the Evangelist and the believers to whom he wrote.

cares, the living as from hand to mouth, the insufficient food and the scanty squalid clothing of the beggar, the trial becomes more wearing, and calls for greater fortitude and faith. We do not sufficiently estimate, I believe, this element in the sufferings of the first believers. Taken for the most part from the humbler class of artisans, often thrown out of employment by the very fact of their conversion, with new claims upon them from the afflicted members of the great family of Christ close at hand or afar off, and a new energy of sacrifice prompting them to admit those claims, subjected not unfrequently to the "spoiling of their goods" (Heb. x. 34), we cannot wonder that they should have had little earthly store, and that their reserve of capital should have been rapidly exhausted. Traces of this meet us, though they are not put forward ostentatiously, in many scattered passages of the New Testament writings. Collections for the poor saints at Jerusalem were made in all the churches of the Gentiles. Those who gave most liberally to that work did so out of the "deep poverty" in which they were themselves plunged, "to the utmost of their power, yea, and beyond their power" (2 Cor. viii. 2, 3). Even the stress laid in some of St. Paul's

Epistles on the duties of the rich points to their position as altogether exceptional. And poverty brought with it, as the Epistle of St. James shews us, some trials to which those who had been devout Israelites before their conversion, and who had not ceased to claim their position as such, would be peculiarly sensitive. In the synagogue which they had been in the habit of attending, and which there was no reason for their at once forsaking, perhaps even in the assemblies of Jewish disciples which still retained the old name and many of the old usages, they would find themselves scorned and scoffed at, thrust into the background, below the footstool of the opulent traders in whom a city like Smyrna was certain to abound (James ii. 2, 3). The hatred which the unbelieving Jews felt for the name of Christ would connect itself with their purse-proud scorn of the poor and needy, and "those beggars of Christians" would become a by-word of reproach.[1]

It was a message of comfort to those who were smarting under that taunt to hear, as from their Lord's lips, "*I know thy poverty,*

---

[1] I may recall to the reader's memory that this is the most accepted explanation of the name Ebionites ("the poor"), applied to a large section of Jewish Christians in the first century.

but thou art rich." He measured poverty and riches by another standard than the world's, and so the words recorded by St. John are, as it were, the echo of those which the brother of the Lord had addressed to men who were in a like condition: " Hath not God chosen the poor of this world rich in faith, and heirs of the kingdom which he hath promised to them that love him?" (James ii. 5.) And He, looking upon their works and their tribulation, knew that they had their treasure in heaven, that they were rich with His own unsearchable riches, that they had laid up their wealth where neither rust nor moth corrupt and where thieves do not break through and steal. Their state was the very antithesis of that which we shall afterwards find described as that of the Church of Laodicea, and in that deep poverty of theirs they were wealthy, beyond the dreams of avarice, in the " gold tried in the fire."

The stress thus laid on one special incident of the tribulation of the Church of Smyrna prepares us to understand the words that follow. I take the blasphemy of which they speak as coming from *"those who say they are Jews and are not,"* as meaning, primarily, not direct blasphemy against God, but the words of reviling which were hurled in reckless scorn at the believers in the name of Christ. It was in the synagogue that they heard the words which reproached them as Nazarenes, Galileans, Christians, disciples of the Crucified; and, as in the case of those of whom St. James writes, those who despised the poor, and whose contempt was aggravated by the fact that these poor were Christians, in reviling them "blasphemed also that worthy name" by which they had been called (James ii. 7). Upon all such, whether they were Jews continuing still in their unbelief, or, as is possible, professing some kind of faith in Christ, yet retaining all the vices of their original Pharisaism, the Lord of the Churches pronounces the sentence that they are no true Jews, that they do not belong to the Israel of God, that the synagogue of which they are the members is nothing else than the synagogue of Satan. His spirit was working in them, the spirit of pride, and hatred, and scorn, and unbelief, and it was well that they, who knew not what manner of spirit they were of, should have their eyes opened to the perils of their true state.

And then there came words which at once told them that they had to face evils that were greater than any they had as yet experienced, and enabled them to bear them. The storm was not yet over. They had but heard its mutterings and seen its distant flashes as compared with the violence with which it was about to break on them. "*The devil*"—for the antagonism to the Truth is traced up here, as elsewhere, beyond all merely human instruments, to the great enemy of God and man, the great accuser and slanderer, the head of all the human *diaboli* who made themselves instruments in his work — would "*cast some of them into prison*," and from that prison some of them should pass out to encounter death in all the manifold forms which the cruelty of their persecutors could devise. They were to be tried with this fiery trial that the gold of their true treasure might be at once tested and purified. That which was designed by their great foe as a temptation leading them to apostasy should work, like all the other "manifold temptations" to which they were exposed, so as to be fruitful in all joy.

The specific mention of the "*ten days*" during which the tribulation was to last has naturally suggested many questions. Are the days to be taken literally, and has the prediction therefore the character of a promise, encouraging the sufferers to stedfastness on the ground of the short duration of the trial? Are we to adopt what has almost come to be assumed as an axiom to the interpretation of other parts of the Apocalypse, that a day stands for a year, and that the words point therefore to the persecution as at once severe and protracted, and calling for the faith which alone endureth to the end? Without adopting, or even for the present discussing, the "year-day" theory, I am disposed to accept the latter view in its general bearing. The number Ten, the last of the scale of numbers, the total of the first four units, each of which had a mystic meaning of its own, is naturally, in the symbolism of numbers, the representative of completeness, and here, therefore, of persecution carried to its full extent, and lacking nothing that could make it thorough and perfect, as a test.[1] It comes as the climax of the whole picture of the sufferings to which the Church of Smyrna was to be exposed. It implies the "death" which is prominently brought forward in the words of promise that follow. In those words we may perhaps find something of a local colouring, imagery drawn from the associations that were necessarily familiar to the Church of

---

[1] The usage of the Old Testament is not consistent. In Gen. xxxi. 41, Num. xiv. 24, Job. xix. 3, the definite number is used to convey the idea of indefinitely frequent repetition. In Gen. xxiv. 58, Num. xi. 19, it is used, apparently, in its literal sense. The interpretation now given is based upon Bähr, *Symbolik*, ii. 2, § 8.

Smyrna and its Angel. In the great games of that city, as in the Isthmian games and those of Olympia, the victor in the strife received the "crown," or "garland" (στέφανος) that was the badge of conquest.[1] For that crown men were ready to endure and dare. It was the great joy and glory of their lives. And such a crown of victory the Lord of the Churches promises to him who is faithful unto death. It is to be "*a crown of life*," the genitive (as in the case of the "crown of righteousness" of 2 Tim. iv. 8) pointing to that of which the crown is, as it were, made up. Life, eternal life, is that which makes the reward of all faithful combatants, and that eternal life con-

[1] Dean Blakesley states, in the article already referred to, but without giving his authority, that the "crown" was given to the priest who presided at the Dionysian mysteries, and that Smyrnæan inscriptions record the names of many persons, men and women, distinguished as στεφανηφόροι. I cannot see any force in the objection urged by Archbishop Trench to this reference, that comparisons drawn from the games of Greece were foreign to the thoughts both of the writer and the readers of the Apocalypse, and that the crowns referred to are therefore the signs, not of victory in conflict, but, like the διαδήματα (diadems) of Rev. xii. 3; xiii. 1; xix. 12, of regal majesty. The Asiatic Churches must have been familiar by this time with the imagery which had been so freely used both by St. Paul (1 Cor. ix. 24–27; 2 Tim. iv. 7; Phil. iii. 13) and the great unknown writer of the Epistle to the Hebrews (Heb. xii. 1); and the fact that St. John uses the other word where the other meaning is required is, at least, presumptive evidence that he uses this in its usual and more definite meaning.

sists in knowing God and Jesus Christ whom He has sent. Now, as ever, He is Himself the exceeding great reward of those who serve Him truly.

The promise with which the message ends, though different and more general, as well as more mystical in its form, expresses substantially the same truth: "*He that overcometh shall not be hurt of the second death.*" The word, so strange and awful, was, so far as we know, comparatively new. Nothing like it meets us in the Gospels, or in the Epistles of St. Peter and St. Paul. And, although we must believe that it had been used before in the teaching of St. John, so that it would not fall on ears to which it would convey no intelligible meaning, it is yet clear that it had not up to this time become part of the current phraseology of the Church.[1] Yet the meaning of the phrase was not far to seek. One who had learnt that the life of the body was not the true life, must have learnt, as the complement of that truth,

[1] The date of the several portions of the Jerusalem Targum to which Archbishop Trench refers as shewing that the word was not strange to Jewish ears, cannot, I believe, be fixed with precision; but it is at least possible that the Jews of Palestine had become familiar with the phrase through the paraphrase given in it of Deut. xxxiii. 6, and Psa. xlix. 11, in which the "second death" is that which comes upon the wicked in the world to come, and is used as synonymous with Gehenna.

that there was a death more terrible than that to which the body is subject—the loss of the eternal life. The teaching of his Lord on earth had indeed implied that "*second death.*" Men were not to fear those who were only able to kill the body, but him who was able to destroy both soul and body in hell (Matt. x. 28). Whosoever believed in Him should not see death, even though his body was committed to the grave; "though he were dead, yet should he live" (John xi. 25). More striking still, as bringing more fully into view the latent terrors of the phrase, is its recurrence in a later chapter of the Revelation. There it is said that the "second death" hath no power over the blessed and holy ones who have part in the first resurrection (xx. 6); and, again, that it is identical with "the lake of fire," into which both Death and Hades are to be cast, together with every one who was not found written in the book of life (xx. 14, 15).

It does not fall within my aim in this volume to enter upon the wide eschatological questions which these passages open as regards the time and sequence of the events thus mysteriously shadowed forth. We are compelled, however, to ask what light they throw upon the promise to the Angel of the Church of Smyrna. Is the "*second death*" to be interpreted by the "lake of fire" as implying a state of enduring pain? Are we to rob the "lake of fire" of its terrors by seeing in it only the "*second death*," of the loss of conscious life or utter annihilation? Here also we stand on the threshold of great problems which we cannot solve. But, as a question of simple interpretation, I am bound to express my conviction that the evidence leads to the former, and not the latter, conclusion. The imagery of the fiery lake, like that of the worm and the flame of the Valley of Hinnom, may be but imagery; but it points at least to some dread reality which is veiled beneath those awful symbols. What that reality is we may infer from St. John's conceptions of the higher life. If the first death is the loss of the first or earthly life, then the second death must be the loss of that knowledge of God which makes the blessedness of eternal life—and that loss is at least compatible with the thought of continuous existence. What possibilities in the far-off future were shadowed forth by the mysterious words that "Death and Hades were cast into the lake of fire," as though they were to be robbed of their power to destroy, and were punished as the great enemies of God and man, how far those who were cast in with them might even there be not shut out from hope, it was not given to the Seer of the Apocalypse to know, nor did he care to ask. It was enough for the faithful sufferers under persecution, who overcame in that conflict with the *plurima mortis imago*, to which they were exposed, to know that this was all that their enemies could inflict on them, and that the "*second death*" should have no power to hurt them.

The date to which I have assigned the Apocalypse, and which gave a special interest to the message to the Church of Ephesus, as being probably addressed to the true son and fellow-worker of St. Paul, deprives me of what would have given an almost equal interest to that now under consideration. I cannot assume with Archbishop Trench and others, whatever latitude I may give to the duration of his life or the date of his conversion, that Polycarp, who suffered martyrdom in A.D. 168, could have been the Angel of the Church of Smyrna at the time when the Apocalypse was written. And yet the coincidences which these writers have pointed out are hardly less interesting on the assumption that though the message was not addressed to him, his life, as a Christian and a pastor, came, more or less, under its influence. In his long conflict for the faith—his stedfast endurance—his estimate of the fire with which men could destroy the body, and the fire that never can be quenched,[1] we find a character on which the promise to him that overcometh had been stamped indelibly. In the narrative of his sufferings, as in the Apocalyptic message, the devil is represented as the great instigator of the persecution of which he was the victim.[2] There also Jews were the most active instruments, as was their manner always, in the fiendish work, even to the point of heaping up the faggots which were to form his funeral pyre.[3]

It is perhaps worth noticing, as shewing the continuance in the Church of Smyrna of the same phraseology as that in the passage before us, that, in the Epistle which purports to be addressed to Polycarp by Ignatius of Antioch, the term "synagogue" is applied to Christian assemblies (C. 4), and that the narrative of the martyrdom ends with describing him as having obtained the crown ($\sigma\tau\acute{\epsilon}\phi\alpha\nu\sigma\varsigma$) of incorruption.[4]

[1] Mart. Polyc. c. 2.
[2] Ibid. c. 3.
[3] Ibid. c. 12, 13.
[4] Ibid. c. 17.

IV.

THE EPISTLE TO PERGAMOS.

THE REVELATION.

CHAPTER II.

12 AND to the angel of the church in Pergamos write; These things saith he which hath the sharp sword with two edges;

13 I know thy works, and where thou dwellest, *even* where Satan's seat *is;* and thou holdest fast my name, and hast not denied my faith, even in those days wherein Antipas *was* my faithful martyr, who was slain among you, where Satan dwelleth.

14 But I have a few things against thee, because thou hast there them that hold the doctrine of Balaam, who taught Balac to cast a stumbling-block before the children of Israel, to eat things sacrificed unto idols, and to commit fornication.

15 So hast thou also them that hold the doctrine of the Nicolaitanes, which thing I hate.

16 Repent; or else I will come unto thee quickly, and will fight against them with the sword of my mouth.

17 He that hath an ear, let him hear what the Spirit saith unto the churches; To him that overcometh will I give to eat of the hidden manna, and will give him a white stone, and in the stone a new name written, which no man knoweth saving he that receiveth *it.*

IV.

IN this instance there seems reason to believe that there is a somewhat closer connection between the outward history of the city and the language in which the Church in that city is described in the Apocalypse than we have found in dealing with the messages to Ephesus and Smyrna. Something there was which gave it a bad eminence over them and over the other cities that are here grouped with it. More emphatically than any other it was the metropolis and fortress of the powers of evil, the place where "*Satan's throne was,*" and where he himself was thought of, as ruling from that throne, as the strong man armed, resenting and resisting the attack which was now made upon him by one mightier than himself. How it came to be so, that outward history may, in part at least, explain.

It is not necessary to go back to the earlier time when the rock citadel of Mysia, about three miles from the banks of the Caicus, first became celebrated for its worship of the mysterious Cabiri, and then, like other sacred places, became a treasury where kings and chieftains deposited their wealth. It will be enough to remember that after the break-up of the Macedonian monarchy it became the capital of a wealthy kingdom, and that Eumenes II. sought to rival the glory of Alexandria by the foundation of a library, in which were stored the chief works of the literature and philosophy of Greece;[1] that it became famous for the worship of the great deities, Zeus, Athene, Dionysos, Apollo, Aphrodite, and, with even a more special devotion, of Æsculapius; that round that last form of idolatry there gathered a great medical school, which was afterwards rendered illustrious by the name of Galen. In this religious character lay its special claim to greatness. It was, as Dean Blakesley has well described it,[2] " a sort of union of a pagan cathedral city, an university town, and a royal residence ;" and when, on the death of Attalus III., it passed, by his bequest, to the Roman Republic, and afterwards to the Empire, it retained its old fame, and was

[1] It may be interesting to some readers to be reminded that from this library we get the name parchment (*charta Pergamena*), as applied to the special kind of vellum that was manufactured for the transcription of its choicest works.

[2] *Dictionary of the Bible*, art. "Pergamos."

described by Pliny as without a rival in the whole province of Asia.

Such a city might well seem to the Apostle to be the headquarters of that great evil Power against which he and his fellow-believers had gone forth in the name of Christ to wage an internecine warfare. And if we picture to ourselves some of the peculiarities of the worship which was there prominent—how Æsculapius was honoured with the name of "Preserver," or "Saviour" ($\Sigma\omega\tau\acute{\eta}\rho$); how in his temple the Æsculapian symbol of the wreathed serpent must have been the most conspicuous object, seeming alike to Jew and Christian to be nothing else but an open adoration of the "great serpent, or dragon, called the Devil and Satan" (Rev. xii. 9); how to them the works of healing that were ascribed to the power of the guardian deity of the city would seem to be lying signs and wonders, and the name which he bore a blasphemous assumption of the power of the true Saviour, and even the books which the followers of Æsculapius studied to be of the class of those belonging to the "curious arts," which they held in righteous abhorrence and which the first fervour of faith had led the zealous converts to destroy (Acts xix. 19)—it will not seem strange that such a city should be described, as we find it described here, as the very throne of Satan, even if there had been no special events to indicate that there the powers of evil were working in their utmost malignity. But the context shews that they had thus displayed themselves. In other cities there had been the trial of persecution, but it had not extended beyond scorn, contumely, spoliation, or, at the furthest, imprisonment, and stripes, and exile. Here it had gone further, and Pergamos had witnessed the death of one whom we may well believe to have been the protomartyr of the Asiatic Churches.

The special intensity of the evils which prevailed at Pergamos determined, it would seem, the choice of the special attribute claimed by the Lord of the Churches as "*He which hath the sharp sword with two edges.*" That sharp sword (the word points, in its literal meaning, to the long sword of the heavy-armed soldier, as distinct from dagger or short sabre) came, it will be remembered, from the mouth, instead of being wielded with the hand, and so answered to the description of the righteous and victorious King given by the prophet (Isa. xi. 4; xlix. 2), and was the symbolic representation of the imagery which the language of St. Paul must have made familiar, and in which the "sword of the Spirit" was "the word of God" (Ephes. vi. 17). As such the two-edged weapon was to do its two-fold work. On the one hand it was to smite that it might heal, "piercing even to the dividing asunder of soul and spirit" (Heb. iv. 12), cutting to the quick, reaching the conscience, laying bare the hidden depths of each man's life. On the other it was also quick and powerful to smite and to destroy; and with it, with the weapon of the Divine Word, the champions of the Truth, and the Captain of the great host of those champions Himself, would win the victory even in that battlefield where the throne of Satan was set up as though he were undisputed lord.

The fact that the Church of Pergamos had witnessed the death of one of its teachers (Antipas) has been already noticed by anticipation: of that "*faithful martyr*" we must be content to confess that we know nothing more than the name. The passing mention of him by Tertullian is obviously drawn from this passage and conveys no information; the longer narrative of Simeon Metaphrastes is as obviously nothing but a martyrdom written to order in the tenth century. The suggestion made by Hengstenberg that the name is itself symbolical; that it is, as it were, equivalent to ἀντίκοσμος, "one who holds his own against every one" (ἀντὶ-πᾶς), an *Athanasius contra Mundum;* and the still wilder conjecture that under this pseudonym we may recognise the living form of Timotheus, though nothing in what the New Testament records connects him with the Pergamene district, may be dismissed as simply and almost childishly fantastic.[1] The name, like that of the Tetrarch of Galilee, is simply a form of Antipatros, as Lucas is of Lucanus, or Zenas of Zenodôrus. And so we must leave the name that thus shines like a star in the firmament of heaven, without knowing more than that he who bore it had, in open conflict against the powers of evil, borne his witness that Christ was the one Healer, Preserver, Saviour, and thus had drawn upon himself the wrath of those who saw their craft endangered, or were roused, apart from motives of interest, to fanatic indignation. It remains only to note that here also the blood of martyrs was the seed of the Church, and was fruitful in a harvest of like noble souls, and that among those who were most conspicuous in the annals of martyrdom in the severer persecutions of the second century were four, at least, who claimed Pergamos as their birthplace.[2]

[1] It may be well to state that I can see nothing in the faint apology which Archbishop Trench makes for Hengstenberg's hypothesis to modify this conviction.

[2] Euseb. *Hist. Eccl.* iv. 15; v. 1.

The words that follow note what there was of evil in the Church in which there was so much that was conspicuously good: "*I have a few things against thee, because thou hast there them that hold the doctrine of Balaam, who taught Balak[1] to cast a stumbling-block before the children of Israel.*" On the assumption to which we were led in examining the reference to the Nicolaitanes in the message to Ephesus, we have here to deal with a distinct form of error. Why the name of Balaam should be the representative of that false doctrine, what was its nature and its practical working, in what relation it stood to the teaching of other parts of the New Testament on the same subject, are all questions of much interest. It will be convenient to deal with the two last first, and to trace the history of the controversy as to εἰδωλόθυτα, or "things sacrificed to idols."

Every convert from Heathenism to the faith of Christ would acknowledge that he was bound to abstain from any participation, direct or indirect, in the false worship which he renounced

---

[1] The anomalous dative τῷ Βάλακ, instead of the accusative common after verbs of teaching, which is found in the better MSS., must, I believe, be explained as an instance of the imperfect knowledge of Greek which led to the use of an idiom more or less Hebraic rather than as a deliberate use of the *dativus commodi*.

at baptism. But the question what acts involved an indirect participation was one that gave rise to a perplexing casuistry, and yet could not be avoided. Was the convert to go out of the world and turn from all social gatherings but those of his own community? Was he to refuse to join in the public meals, at inns or elsewhere, which travel made almost indispensable? If he did so refuse, he cut himself off not only from the pleasures, but from the duties and opportunities of family and social companionship. Yet if he accepted the invitation, there was the risk that he might be eating of the flesh of sheep or ox which the host had himself sacrificed, as a festive thank-offering, to Zeus or Apollo, or that the wine which he drank might have been poured out as a libation. If he did so eat, was he not, in "eating of the sacrifice," a partaker in the worship, eating the flesh and drinking the cup which belonged to the demons that he had learnt to identify with the gods whom the Heathen worshipped? (1 Cor. xi. 20.) Yet another case presented itself which followed the convert even to his own home. Of the sacrifices that were offered in Heathen temples the greater part became the perquisite of the priests. When they had more than they could consume themselves they sold it to the meat-dealers of the market. The Christian convert, therefore, could never be sure that what he bought had not been thus offered, and the sensitive conscience was harassed with the tormenting thought of an unknown and involuntary transgression, which yet brought with it defilement and condemnation. The Jew might avoid the danger by dealing only, as, for the most part, Jews deal now, with a butcher of his own persuasion; but this implied a more settled and organised society than that of most Christian communities in the early days of the Church's life, and many years would probably pass away before the convert was able to meet with a Christian butcher. On the other hand, in most cases, the Jewish butcher would probably refuse to supply him; or, if that were not the case, would only do so under the restrictions (to the Gentile burdensome and vexatious) of the Mosaic law of clean and unclean meats.

How near the surface the question lay is seen by the fact that it occupied an almost co-ordinate place with that of circumcision, and entered into what then appeared as the great charter of the freedom of the Gentile converts. The decision of the Apostles and Elders in that first Council at Jerusalem was practically of the nature of a compromise. On the one hand the converts were released from the necessity of circumcision; on the other, by way of makeweight, they were commanded to "abstain from meats offered to idols, and from blood, and from things strangled, and from fornication" (Acts xv. 20). The grouping of these latter prohibitions was due to the fact that they were popularly recognised as among the precepts of Noah, which were held to be binding upon all his descendants, and were required, therefore, even by the more liberal Rabbis, of all " proselytes of the gate; " while those who aspired to the higher blessedness of the children of Abraham had to qualify themselves as " proselytes of righteousness" by the sign of circumcision. The decree was, as I have said, received at first with a joyous welcome. But soon new difficulties presented themselves as rising out of the broad general language in which it spoke. Did *any* eating of meat that had been sacrificed to idols, even if unconscious, involve the eater in pollution? Others, at a distance from Jerusalem, Gentile converts, reasoning from broad principles to bold conclusions, might question the obligation of that which seemed to rest on no great principle, but to represent a policy of conciliation and concession. If an idol was "nothing in the world," a powerless block of marble or of wood, how could it taint the flesh of the victim sacrificed to it, and make the creature of God, in itself good, unfit for human food? Some, waxing yet bolder, seem to have contended that they might even take their place in a public banquet within the precincts of an idol temple, so long as they were not required to join in any formal act of worship. (1 Cor. viii. 10.)

Such was the state of things which St. Paul found at Corinth. There the more scrupulous party, under the influence of Jewish feeling, was obviously the weaker; the bolder were also the stronger, exulting in their knowledge, their rights, their independence. It is remarkable that, in arguing with these latter, St. Paul never makes even the most distant allusion to the decree of the Council of Jerusalem, though he himself had been at least a consenting party to it. For some reason of policy or principle, because the Corinthians would have demurred to the authority of the Council, or from a characteristic love of going to the bottom of a matter, he discusses the questions of casuistry that thus presented themselves on the ground, not of authority, but of the rights of conscience. Sin lay in the will, and therefore an involuntary act done in ignorance was no transgression;

and as the act was in its own nature neutral, the man need not be over-anxious to ask questions the answer to which might involve him in perplexity. Where, on the other hand, the convert was, as it were, openly challenged or tempted to partake of the sacrificial food, he was to abstain, yielding up the abstract right, which St. Paul fully recognised, lest he should wound the conscience of any other less strong-minded than himself. (1 Cor. x. 21.) For a like reason the Apostle, while apparently admitting, for the sake of argument, the abstract possibility of a blameless participation in a banquet, even in the idol temple, first earnestly dissuades men from it, on the ground of its perilous consequences to others; and then, on what more truly expressed his own convictions, as involving a formal recognition of the false worship which the Christian had renounced in his baptism. (1 Cor. x. 18–21.)

I have dwelt at this length on the position occupied by St. Paul in this controversy because it has been maintained by Renan and other recent writers, who see in the different aspects of teaching presented by the writers of the New Testament Epistles not only diversities of gifts, but antagonism of principles, that the strong language of the Apocalypse is intended to be a condemnation of his teaching; that he is, in fact, the Balaam whom St. John seeks to hold up to the abhorrence of the Churches, just as others have identified him with the Simon Magus who appears as "the hero of the romance of heresy" in the strange controversial novel known as the "Clementine Recognitions."[1] It can, I believe, be shewn that this theory is altogether destitute of probability; that the minds of St. Paul and St. John were in this respect in perfect harmony; that even dealing with the Message as coming *from*, and not *to*, the latter Apostle, it is such as the former would have accepted and rejoiced in.

And (1) I note that those who are condemned by the Message are precisely those whom St. Paul urges, on grounds of a moral expediency so high that it becomes a duty, to refrain from the exercise of the freedom and the right of which they boasted. It was to be expected that some in their self-will would harden themselves against the appeal; that they might even use St. Paul's name, and boast that they were more

[1] Comp. Renan's "St. Paul." "Les chapitres ii. et iii. de l'Apocalypse sont un cri de haine contre Paul et ses amis," p. 367. So assuming that Balaam is translated into Nicolas, "un seducteur paien, qui eut des visions quoique infidèle, un homme qui engageant le peuple à pécher avec filles des paiennes, parut le vrai type de Paul," p. 304.

consistent with his principles than he was himself. This, we know, was what Marcion and his followers actually did when they claimed a like liberty for themselves; and Marcion may well have had forerunners among the Gnostics of the apostolic age. And it would be but natural that those who took this attitude towards one of the restrictions imposed by the Council at Jerusalem should act in like manner towards another, and look at the sin of fornication from the Heathen, and not from the Jewish or the Christian, point of view, as a thing in itself indifferent; a sensual pleasure, it was true, but not more worthy of blame than that of eating meat that had been offered in sacrifice to idols, or food which the Jewish law prohibited as unclean. The very grouping of the apostolic decree might seem at first sight to favour the view that the prohibitions were of co-ordinate obligation. The earnestness with which St. Paul warns the Corinthians against falling back into the old vicious habits in which they had once indulged with no consciousness of sin, the passing reference (1 Cor. vi. 13) to "meats for the belly and the belly for meats," in connection with those habits, shew how closely the two were connected in his own mind and in the influences that were at work in the Church to which he wrote. The habitual license of the orgies of many Heathen festivals, the prevalence of prostitution in the precincts of many temples, the presence, in that of Aphrodite, of the harlot priestesses who made Corinth infamous, all brought the two evils of which St. Paul wrote into very close combination.

(2) It must be remembered that the strange prominence given to the name of Balaam in the later writings of the New Testament began, not with the real or supposed anti-Pauline teachers, but with that Apostle himself. It was in his warnings to the Corinthians (1 Cor. x. 8) that that dark history of the days when Israel abode in Shittim was first recalled to the memory of the Christian Church: "Neither let us commit fornication, as some of them committed, and fell in one day three and twenty thousand." Then, as in later days, the two sins had gone together, and the Israelites had both committed whoredom with the daughters of Moab and joined themselves to Baal-peor, and eaten the sacrifices of their gods (Num. xxv. 1-3). When St. Peter,[1] then, speaks of the false

---

[1] I assume the genuineness of the second Epistle that bears the name of Peter; but it makes no difference in my argument if it is treated as an instance of pseudonymous authorship.

teachers, who had "eyes full of adultery" and beguiled unstable souls," as following the way of Balaam the son of Bosor (2 Pet. ii. 14, 15); when St. Jude describes those who "corrupt themselves in what they know naturally as brute beasts" as "going greedily after the error of Balaam for reward;" when St. John records the condemnation of those "*that hold the doctrine of Balaam, who taught Balak to cast a stumbling-block before the children of Israel, to eat things sacrificed unto idols, and to commit fornication,*" they are not glancing obliquely and with the glance of hate at the teaching of St. Paul, but are actually echoing it.

(3) It may be noted, as accounting for the stronger and more vehement language of the Apocalypse, considered even as a simply human book, that the conditions of the case had altered. Christians and Heathens were no longer dwelling together, as at Corinth, with comparatively slight interruption to their social interco but were divided by a sharp line of demarc The eating of things sacrificed to idols was and more a crucial test, involving a shrinking from the open confession of a tian's faith. Disciples who sat at meat in the idol's temple were making merry with th

whose hands were red with the blood of their fellow-worshippers and whose lips had uttered blaspheming scoffs against the Holy Name.

And to this teaching, as to the kindred doctrine of the Nicolaitanes,[1] arriving at the same goal by a different path, o'erleaping itself from an overstrained asceticism and falling on the other side, scorning the body, and therefore indifferent to its acts, the Angel of the Church of Pergamos had offered but a feeble and slack resistance. There was no righteous hatred such as won the praise of his Lord for the Angel of the Church of Ephesus. Tolerance of these debasing forms of evil took its place among the "*few things*" for which he was reproved. And a sharp warning both for himself and for the false teachers followed on the reproof: "*Repent, else I will come to thee quickly, and will fight against them with the sword of my mouth.*" There is, it will be seen, a marked distinction between the two clauses. To the chief pastor of the church, in his separate personal responsibility for his moral feebleness, the Lord "*comes quickly.*" The words are important as shewing that "*coming quickly*" had, in the mind

---

[1] I have already expressed my dissent from the view that the Nicolaitanes were identical with the followers of Balaam. The view given in the text seems to me the nearest approximation possible to their real relations to each other.

of the Apostle, quite another meaning besides that of the great final Advent. In ways which the man reproved would feel, in the chances and changes of life, in failure and disappointment, in suffering and shame, He would visit the offending pastor who did not repent and rouse himself to a nobler energy from conviction. But with the others he would "*make war with the sword of his mouth.* There may be in this, as many have thought, a reference to the fact that Balaam the son of Beor was slain with the sword of the children of Israel, which was also the sword of God; but I agree with Alford in thinking that this reference is, to say the least, remote, and that the words receive a sufficient explanation from the imagery of the immediate context. And if, as we have seen, the sword of the Spirit is here also the Word of God,—that which cometh from the mouth of the Lord,—then we may well adopt the interpretation given by Grotius as leading us to the true and spiritual meaning of the passage. In that warfare the weapons would not be carnal. He, the Lord, would raise up faithful and true prophets, and his word should be in their mouths also as a sharp sword, and they would wield that sword effectively and slay the monstrous forms of error that were warring against the truth.

The promise "*to him that overcometh*" presents in this case points at once of peculiar difficulty and special interest. The meaning of the "*manna*" appears, perhaps, at first not far to seek. Those who remember with what fulness St. John, and he alone, records the teaching in which his Master claimed to be the Bread of God, the living bread that came down from heaven, of which, if a man ate, he should live for ever, as contrasted with the manna in the wilderness, which had no power to save from death (John vi. 33, 50), will be ready to admit that the words now before us must have recalled that teaching, and that the manna which was to be the reward of the conqueror was the fruition of the ineffable sweetness of that divine Presence. Those who resisted the temptation to join the idol's feast in the idol's temple should be admitted to that heavenly feast in the eternal temple, which was also the palace of the great King. But the epithet "*hidden*" suggests more than this. In the current belief of the Jews the sacred treasures of the Temple, which had disappeared when Jerusalem was laid waste by the army of the Chaldeans, had not been allowed to perish. The Prophet Jeremiah had carried them to "the mountain, where Moses climbed up and saw the heritage of God"

(2 Macc. ii. 4), *i.e.* the heights of Pisgah, and there they were kept, no man knowing of the place, "until the time that God shall gather his people again together and shew them his mercy." It was not strange that the imagination of devout Jews should dwell on that legend, and picture to themselves the restoration, not only of the Shekinah and the Urim and the Thummim, and the ark and the tables of stone, but also of the manna that had been thus hidden. This, and the general thought that the hidden and the precious were, for the most part, co-extensive terms (as in Psa. xvii. 14, "Whose bellies thou fillest with thy *hid* treasures"), will explain why the word was chosen to heighten all that was conveyed by the promise of the manna. Whatever men had dreamt of blessedness and joy should be surpassed by the taste of that "*hidden* manna," the gladness of that life which is "*hid* with Christ in God" (Col. iii. 3).

The "*white stone, and the new name written on it, which no man knoweth saving he that receiveth it,*" present difficulties of another kind, chiefly, as by a strange paradox, through the very ease with which they admit of interpretations more or less probable. In the symbolism of colours, which, as having its ultimate root in impressions of pain or pleasure made upon the senses, might almost be called natural, and is, as a matter of fact, all but universal, white, in its brightness and purity, had been associated with joy and gladness, with victory and triumph. So, in a practice which, though originating, it was said, with the half-civilised tribes of Thrace or Scythia, had become general, days of festivity were noted with a white, those of calamity with a black, stone. So, when the vote of an assembly as to the guilt of an accused person was taken by ballot, white stones were the symbol of an acquittal, black of a condemnation. It has, accordingly, been contended, with at least much plausibility, that this is the significance of the "white stone" in the promise now before us. The conqueror in the great strife with evil, whatever opprobrium he might incur in the sight of men, whatever sentence he might receive at the hands of an earthly judge, would be received as justified and acquitted by the Eternal Judge. Yet, on the other hand, it can scarcely be said that the symbol of a mere acquittal would be an adequate expression of the reward promised to him that overcometh. A verdict of "not guilty," which, on this interpretation, would exhaust the meaning of the promise, could hardly take its place as co-ordinate with the "crown of life," or with "*the tree of life which is in the midst of the paradise of God.*"

Partly on the ground of this inadequacy, partly on the general principle that the source of the Apocalyptic imagery must be sought, not in the customs of Heathen antiquity, but in the more venerable symbolism of the Jewish ritual, it has been contended by Archbishop Trench, following a German commentator (Zullig), that the "white stone," associated as it is with one of the lost treasures of the sanctuary of Israel, must be interpreted as another of those treasures, and be identified accordingly with the Urim and Thummim of the High Priest's vestments, on the assumption that they consisted of one or more stones of translucent and colourless purity, of the nature of diamond or rock crystal. There is so much in this view of these "stones oracular" that commends itself to me, that it is not without reluctance I am brought to the conviction, as I have elsewhere shewn,[1] that it is not applicable to the passage now before us. Not only were the Urim and Thummim almost or altogether beyond the horizon of the thoughts of the writers of the New Testament, so that throughout its pages there is not a single allusion to them, not even where we should have

[1] *Dictionary of the Bible*, art. "Urim and Thummin."

most looked for it, in the Epistle to the Hebrews, unless it be in this obscure and debateable passage; but the word used by St. John is not that which throughout the LXX. and the New Testament is used of precious stones and gems (λίθος), but that which describes the secondary and derived use of stones or pebbles in social or political life (ψῆφος). On these grounds it seems to me that there is a strong *primâ facie* presumption against Archbishop Trench's view; nor can I admit that it is counterbalanced by the view (which I have shewn, in dealing with the message to the Church of Smyrna, to be unproven) that all allusions to Heathen usages are outside the circle of Apocalyptic symbolism. On the whole, then, with one important modification, I am disposed to adopt Ewald's view, who sees in the stone, or ψῆφος of the promise, the *tessera hospitalis*, by which, in virtue of form or characters inscribed on it, he who possessed it could claim from the friend who gave it, at any distance of time, a frank and hearty welcome. What I would suggest, as an addition to this, rises out of the probability, almost the certainty, that some such *tessera*, or ticket—a stone with the name of the guest written on it—was given to those who were invited to partake, within the precincts of the temple, of the feast that consisted wholly, or in part, of the meat that had been offered as a sacrifice.[1] On this view, the second part of the promise is brought into harmony with the first, and is made more directly appropriate: he who had the courage to refuse that *tessera* to the feast that defiled should receive another that would admit him to the supper of the Great King.

This hypothesis gives, it will be seen at once, a fresh vividness to the closing words which speak of the "*new name*" that was to be written on it. Here we are at once within the circle of familiar prophetic language. The "*new name*" had been to Isaiah and Jeremiah the formula for expressing the new life of blessedness in store for those to whom it was applied. The land that had been forsaken and abandoned to destruction should be called "Hephzibah," as once more the delight of her Lord. The daughter of Zion, that had sat desolate as a widow, should be "Beulah," as a bride over whom the bridegroom once more rejoiced (Isa. lxii. 2-4; comp. lxv. 15). Jerusalem herself was to be known by the

---

[1] Some such *tessera*, giving the bearer admission to the theatre of Dionysos at Athens, are, if I remember rightly, to be seen among the Greek antiquities of the British Museum.

mystic name of the "Lord our Righteousness" (Jer. xxxiii. 16). In his own case and that of his brother, as in that of Simon Barjona—in Peter, the "Rock," and Boanerges, the "Sons of Thunder"—the Apostle had known a new name given which was the symbol of a higher life and a character idealised in its gifts. And so in this case the inner truth, that lies below the outward imagery, would seem to be that the conqueror, when received at the heavenly feast, should find upon the stone, or *tessera*, that gave him the right of entrance, a "new name," the token of a character transformed and perfected, a name the full significance of which should be known only to him who was conscious of the transformation, just as in the experiences of our human life, "the heart knoweth his own bitterness, and the stranger doth not intermeddle with his joy" (Prov. xiv. 10).

The apparent parallelism of the description in chap. xix. of Him who "was called Faithful and True," whose "name was called the Word of God," and who yet had besides "these a name written that no man knew but he himself" (xix. 11-13), has led some interpreters to suppose that here also it is the name of the Lord, new, wonderful, mysterious, as expressing some relation between Him and his people which the names as yet revealed do not perfectly embody, that is promised to him that overcometh. A closer study of the parallelism will, however, I believe, confirm the view which has been given above. As the Lord alone knows the name which He bears, so the name written upon the stone given to the conqueror is known only to him that receiveth it. What is this but the expression, in the language of symbolism, of the truth which the writer of the Apocalypse expressed afterwards in language more purely abstract and ideal: "Now are we the sons of God, and it doth not yet appear what we shall be: but we know that, when he shall appear, we shall be like him: for we shall see him as he is"? (1 John iii. 2.) Only when humanity has become partaker of the Divine nature will it be able to comprehend the mystery of His being who is at once divine and human. And yet in that likeness of all the saved to their common Lord there shall be no mere uniformity. There, also, as the manna in the Jewish legends was said to taste to each man like the food in which he most delighted, each soul shall recognise in the work which Christ has done for it that of which none can know the wonder nor the sweetness but himself.

V.

THE EPISTLE TO THYATIRA.

THE REVELATION.

CHAPTER II.

18 AND unto the angel of the church in Thyatira write; These things saith the Son of God, who hath his eyes like unto a flame of fire, and his feet *are* like fine brass;

19 I know thy works, and charity, and service, and faith, and thy patience, and thy works; and the last *to be* more than the first.

20 Notwithstanding I have a few things against thee, because thou sufferest that woman Jezebel, which calleth herself a prophetess, to teach and to seduce my servants to commit fornication, and to eat things sacrificed unto idols.

21 And I gave her space to repent of her fornication; and she repented not.

22 Behold, I will cast her into a bed, and them that commit adultery with her into great tribulation, except they repent of their deeds.

23 And I will kill her children with death; and all the churches shall know that I am he which searcheth the reins and hearts: and I will give unto every one of you according to your works.

24 But unto you I say, and unto the rest in Thyatira, as many as have not this doctrine, and which have not known the depths of Satan, as they speak; I will put upon you none other burden.

25 But that which ye have *already* hold fast till I come.

26 And he that overcometh, and keepeth my works unto the end, to him will I give power over the nations:

27 And he shall rule them with a rod of iron; as the vessels of a potter shall they be broken to shivers: even as I received of my Father.

28 And I will give him the morning star.

29 He that hath an ear, let him hear what the Spirit saith unto the churches.

V.

LITTLE as we know of the general history of this Church in the apostolic age, it has at least one point of contact with the record of the life and labours of St. Paul. The purple-seller of the city of Thyatira, who went with other women to "the place where prayer was wont to be made," to the oratory by the riverside at Philippi, and "whose heart the Lord opened that she attended unto the things that were spoken of Paul" (Acts xvi. 14), is among the most familiar figures in St. Luke's history of the mission-work of the Church. The facts that connect themselves with that mention of her name are also so generally known that it will not be necessary to do more than briefly refer to them.

(1) Thyatira, situated geographically, as it stands in the order of the Messages, between Pergamos and Sardis, owed, if not its origin, yet its importance to the fact of its being one of the Macedonian colonies founded by Alexander the

Great after his conquest of the Persian Empire. As such, it was natural, even after the lapse of three centuries, that it should have many links that connected it with the mother country, and of this the presence of Lydia at Philippi may fairly be taken as an instance. (2) Inscriptions, the date of which is referred to the period between Vespasian and Caracalla, shew that the city contained many corporate guilds, which were united together by common pursuits and religious rites, and that of these the guild of dyers was one of the most prominent. That art was indeed common to a good many of the Asiatic cities, and the commercial fame of Miletus in particular mainly rested on it; but of all these, Thyatira was the only one that had any connection with Macedonia. When we meet with Lydia at Philippi, she is already "one that worshipped God," a half-proselyte, *i.e.* to Judaism; and we may reasonably infer from this the presence of a Jewish element, more or less influential, among the population of the city from which she came. The inhabitants seem indeed to have presented, from the names that appear on their monuments, a greater mingling of races than was commonly to be found, and included Macedonians, Italians, Asiatics (in the narrower sense of that word as including the inhabitants of the Proconsular province of Asia), and Chaldæans. The chief object of their cultus was Apollo, worshipped as the Sun-God, under the Macedonian name of Tyrinnas.

It has been suggested by Dean Blakesley here, as before in the case of Smyrna, that the special words by which the Lord of the Churches describes Himself were determined by the character of the worship just referred to. He assumes that there was a statue of Apollo, of gold and ivory, or of wood or marble richly gilt; that this shone with a dazzling brightness, and that the "*eyes like a flame of fire and the feet like fine brass*" were meant to present the image of the Lord of the Churches as yet more glorious and terrible. Ingenious as the conjecture is, it has, I believe, nothing but its ingenuity to commend it. The imagery had been already used without reference to any local colouring, and a reason for this special application of it may be found in the aspects of stern sovereignty which marks the whole Message. The feet of *chalcolibanus* shall crush the enemies of God as though they were the vessels of a potter.

The special notes of praise assigned to the Church of Thyatira correspond in a very marked degree with those which we find prominent also in the character of the Philippians. Loving ministrations, patient endurance, warm-hearted faith, the more feminine graces of the perfect Christian character are dominant in both. It has been held by not a few writers (notably by Canon Lightfoot) that this characteristic of the Philippian converts was, in part, owing to the continued influence of the first European proselyte in that Church.[1] If we remember that she came from Thyatira, and not improbably returned to it after a season, it is at least interesting to trace there also the same type of character as having been developed possibly under the same influence. And there were no signs of any falling off in this respect. The "last works" were "more than the first." What was wanted was that these graces should be balanced by others of a more masculine type, by righteous zeal against evil, by the exercise, when necessary, of the power to judge and to condemn. Here also the prayer of one who knew what the Church needed would have been that their "love might abound more and more in knowledge and in all judgment" (Phil. i. 9).

We cannot enter on the words which follow without noticing the strange reading, not "*that*

---

[1] See also a Paper on "The Sisterhood at Philippi," in the present writer's *Biblical Studies*.

woman," but "*thy wife, Jezebel*" (τὴν γυναῖκα σου), which would force upon us the conclusion that the work of the Angel, or Bishop, of the Church of Thyatira was thwarted by one who ought to have been his helpmate in it; that she had become tainted with the teaching of the followers of Balaam, and claimed as a prophetess an authority that over-ruled her husband's. I cannot set aside that reading on account of the strangeness of the picture thus presented to us, for truth is often stranger than fiction.[1] And on the principle, which has become almost an axiom in textual criticism, that the more difficult reading is probably the true one, this, com-

---

[1] If we receive this reading, we find (as Dr. Wordsworth has pointed out) a singular parallel in the Epistle of Polycarp to the Philippian Church (c. xi). There also the influence of women, at first, as we have seen, an element for good, had become the source of evil; and the wife of a presbyter named Valens is mentioned as having encouraged him in his transgressions. Strangely enough, too, the transgression is like in kind to that with which the Message to Thyatira deals. We have indeed only the Latin text of this part of the Epistle, and there we read: "Moneo itaque vos, ut abstineatis ab avaritiâ et sitis casti, et veraces. . . . Si quis non abstinuerit ab avaritia, ab idololatria coinquinabitur." The "avaritia" of the Latin corresponds, however, in all probability, to the Greek πλεονεξία, and that word, as in 1 Thess. iv. 5, and probably in 1 Cor. v. 10, was used in a secondary sense, as implying the lawless lust which was regardless of the rights of others. The union of the "avaritia" with "idololatria" almost forces this meaning upon us, and so presents the two as being in as close an alliance at Philippi as at Thyatira.

mended as it is by some of the highest MSS., may well claim admission into the text. We can understand the deliberate suppression of a fact so startling. It is hard to understand the deliberate insertion of a word that would create so great a difficulty. On the other hand, it must be remembered that there is hardly any limit to be set to the blunders, pure and simple, of transcribers, and that the pronoun which creates the perplexity is wanting in at least one (the Sinaitic MS.) of the first-class authorities.

On the whole, then, it seems best to deal with the passage, in any case sufficiently startling, without the additional element of strangeness which this reading gives it. I cannot, however, accept the view taken by Alford and others, that "the woman Jezebel" represents, not a person, but a sect. Everything in the description has, if I mistake not, a distinctly individualising character, and as such it throws light on some interesting social questions connected with the history of the Apostolic Church.

It lay in the nature of the Pentecostal gift that the powers which it conferred were not confined to one sex any more than to one class or race. Daughters as well as sons were to prophesy; the Spirit was to be poured on the "handmaids" as well as the "servants" of the

Lord. (Acts ii. 17, 18.) In Palestine, doubtless, the exercise of these gifts would be restricted by what had become, in spite of the older recollections of Deborah and Huldah, the traditional position of women in the religious life. It was not likely that a woman would be bold enough to speak in a synagogue where all of her own sex were screened off from seeing or being seen. In Greek-speaking countries, on the other hand, familiar with the thought of Sibyls and Pythian priestesses and damsels like that at Philippi with a spirit of divination (Acts xvi. 16), the true gift would more readily find a sphere of action, and would be more exposed, on the one hand, to the excitement and ecstasy which were among the incidents of its working; and, on the other, to the rivalry of a counterfeit inspiration, morbid in its nature, presenting phenomena of startling extravagance and easily enlisted in support of the wild imaginings which were the germs of heresy. Traces of that extravagance we meet with in the Church of Corinth. Women had appeared in the public gatherings of the Church, and had "prophesied" with their faces unveiled, casting aside that which, both in the Jewish and Greek code of social ethics, was the symbol of womanly reserve. (1 Cor. xi. 5-10.) At first, it would seem, St. Paul had been content to reprove any manifestation of the prophetic power that was accompanied by so flagrant a disregard of the principles which, then as always, were the foundation of the rules of conventional decorum. But second thoughts (I do not think it irreverent to attribute second thoughts even to an apostle) led him to the conclusion that the risks of abuse were so great that it was better to restrain the practice which was so liable to them; and accordingly, both in a later chapter of the same Epistle (1 Cor. xiv. 34, 35) and in the injunctions which he left as his last bequest to the Asiatic Churches (1 Tim. ii. 11, 12), he laid down the rule that women were to be "silent" in all assemblies of the Church at which men were present, and to confine the exercise of their gifts to the work of teaching their own sex. We know too little of the conditions under which the four daughters of Philip the Evangelist prophesied at Cæsarea (Acts xxi. 8) to be able to say whether this was an exception to St. Paul's rule. It is probable enough that it was only in the privacy of their own home, or surrounded by female disciples, that they gave utterance to the words which came from their lips, instinct with a divine power; it is possible that their character as "virgins" (*i.e.* not merely unmarried women,

The Epistle to Thyatira. 141

but consecrated to a ministerial life) gained for them exceptional privileges; it is possible, lastly, that the Apostolic Churches were not bound by any uniform code of rules and rubrics, and that that of Cæsarea had not as yet adopted the regulation which was binding on the Churches founded by St. Paul.

What we have to deal with, in any case, in the Church of Thyatira is the assumption, on the part of some conspicuous woman, possibly, as has been said, the wife of the Bishop or Angel of the Church, of the character of a prophetess, supported by the phenomena that simulated inspiration, and that her utterances were used to support the twofold errors of the Nicolaitanes and the followers of Balaam, "*to teach and to seduce*" the servants of Christ "*to commit fornication, and to eat things sacrificed to idols.*" The name of Jezebel, the representative of the Zidonian worship which had tainted the life of Israel with its impurities, was used, as that of Balaam had been, to point the sharpness of the rebuke, possibly with a special reference to the memorable scene when she, with unveiled face, and the brightness of her eyes heightened with the *kohl* of Eastern cosmetics, looked out of her palace window to try for the last time her powers of fascination, or, if those failed, of defiance, on the advancing conqueror and avenger (2 Kings ix. 30). It would hardly be at variance with what we know of the workings of the unrestrained orgiastic impulse at other times and in other countries (as, *e.g.*, in the Bacchanalia, of which Livy, xxxix. 8-19, gives so terrible a description) to assume that the words of verse 22 were literally true; and that here too the Agapæ, or love-feasts of the Chistian Church, were stained, as the hints in 2 Peter ii. 13, 14, and Jude, verse 12, not obscurely intimate, with the perpetration of fathomless impurities in which this so-called prophetess was herself a sharer.

The words of threatening that follow on the statement of the guilt were not less distinctly personal in their character. As the incestuous adulterer at Corinth was delivered to Satan for the destruction of the flesh that the spirit might be saved in the day of the Lord (1 Cor. v. 5); as those who polluted the Supper of the Lord with riotous excess received not only the just reward, but the natural fruit of their sin, in sickness and in death (1 Cor. xi. 30), so it was here. The penal discipline of sickness was needed to wake up the self-blinded prophetess to perceive the real character of the evil into which she had plunged; and she was to be "*cast into the bed*" of pain and weariness; and those that were sharers in her guilt into "*great tribulation*," while "*her children*" were to be "*slain with death*." The received explanation of the last clause is that the "children" of the false prophetess were her followers and supporters; and for those who maintain the impersonal character of the woman Jezebel, as representing a wild heretical sect, such an interpretation is, of course, at once natural and inevitable. It is hard, however, to distinguish, on this hypothesis, between the "*children*" and "*those that commit fornication with her*," in their different degrees of complicity; and, on the whole, I see no reason for abandoning the literal meaning even here. The writers of the New Testament recognised, as we have seen, in the events of life a divine order, sometimes a divine interposition; and as the death of the child of sin had been the appropriate penalty of David's great transgression (2 Sam. xii. 14), so it might be here. The loss of "the desire of her eyes," the death of the children who were the issue of her shameless life, was to be the sharpest pang in the penal discipline that was to come on her; and, stript and bare of all that once made the joy of life, weary and sick, without the smiles of children round her, the false prophetess was to await her end. So should all the Churches know that the Lord was "*he which searcheth the hearts and reins,*" discerning all the baseness and impurity which were clothed with the high-sounding swelling words of knowledge, wisdom, freedom; that, though the long-suffering of God may in many cases reserve the execution of his sentence till the term of probation is over, there are yet others in which the sins of men bring on themselves a swift destruction, and that they which sow to the flesh shall of the flesh reap corruption.

Another characteristic feature of the false teaching of these early Gnostics appears in the words that follow. They boasted that they alone had the courage and the power to know the "depths of Satan." The peculiar addition, "*as they say,*" indicates that the phrase was one in frequent use among them, and it throws light on the relation in which they stood to the great teachers of the Apostolic Church. Here, as in the matter of eating things sacrificed to idols, they were caricaturing and perverting the language of St. Paul. From him, after he had tracked the mysterious working of the divine love in permitting evil for the sake of a greater good, had burst the rapturous cry, "Oh, the *depth* of the riches both of the wisdom and knowledge of God" (Rom. xi. 33). He, in contemplating the glory which eye had not seen, nor ear heard, but which God had revealed by his Spirit, had spoken of that Spirit thus working in man as one that "searcheth all things, even the *deep* things of God" (1 Cor. ii. 10). It was, in the nature of things, probable that those who claimed a prophetic inspiration, shewing itself in a higher form of knowledge than that which was given to others, should take up a phrase so congenial to their boastful claims, and talk much of their acquaintance with the "depths of God." If their boasts were limited to that knowledge, we must see in the startling phrase the "*depths of Satan*," the stern irony of condemnation. Their fancied knowledge of the mysteries of the Divine Nature, obtained by a deliberate transgression of every divine commandment, did but bring them nearer to that Satanic nature, in which knowledge without holiness was seen in its highest power. As those who called themselves Jews were of "*the synagogue of Satan*," as those who boasted of their freedom were themselves the servants of corruption, so was it here. Every step they took that led them further into the depths of a mystic impurity did but identify them with that Power of evil which Christ had come to conquer and destroy. It is possible, however, and the position of the words "*as they say*" renders it even probable, that their dark imaginings carried them even to the literal utterance of the words which are put, as it were, into their lips. We cannot conquer Satan, they may have said, so long as we are ignorant of any of his devices: we must enlarge the range of our experience till we have fathomed the depths of evil and emerged from them uninjured; we must shew that though the body may be sharer in all that men count impure, it may yet leave the spirit with a clear and unclouded vision of the things of God. That form of Antinomianism has too many parallels in the history of human error for us to think it incredible that it should have appeared in a soil so fruitful in all strange dreams of morbid fancy as that of the Asiatic Churches; and we need not wonder if a delusion to which the language, though not the life, even of a Luther at times drew perilously near, which has been the leading idea of life to not a few of the world's greatest poets, exercised its horrible fascination when it came from the lips of the false prophetess of Thyatira.

As the word "*depth*" gave us the key to the

meaning of this part of the Message, so does the word "*burden*" to that of the part which follows: "*I will put upon you none other burden but that which ye have already; hold fast till I come.*" The Apostle hears from his Lord the echo of that decree to which he had once been a consenting party. "It seemed good to the Holy Ghost and to us to lay upon you no greater *burden* than these necessary things" (Acts xv. 28). They might ask, as they heard this reproof of the freedom and the license which they claimed as boasting to be the true representatives of St. Paul's teaching, more Pauline than St. Paul himself, "Are we then to be brought once again under the yoke of bondage? Is the Law, with all its restraints and prohibitions, to be once more the code of the Church of Christ?" To such questions the words which the Seer wrote supplied the answer: "No; that which you once welcomed as the great charter of your freedom has not been cancelled. You may have all the liberty which it permits. No other burden is to be imposed upon you—neither circumcision, nor that which circumcision implies. But that charter contained, in precise terms, the command to abstain from eating things sacrificed to idols, and from fornication; and these rules of life are still binding, as in accordance with the mind of Christ; the first as resting on the duty of witnessing for Christ, and the second as founded on the eternal law of purity. Keep that fast through all trials and temptations till I come, and then he that overcometh shall receive his due reward."

The nature of that reward in this instance is described in terms of singular grandeur: "*I will give him authority* [ἐξουσία, the might of right, not δύναμις, the right of might] *over the Gentiles, and he shall guide them*[1] [ποιμανεῖ, shall do a shepherd's work] *with a rod of iron; as the vessels of a potter shall they be broken in pieces, even as I have received of my Father.*" The promise is nothing less than that the faithful victor shall be a sharer in the sovereignty of the Anointed King, as described in the great Messianic prophecy of Psa. ii. 9. There is, we cannot but believe, the same special adaptation in this case, as in the others, of the promised reward to the peculiar circumstances of the conflict. That to which

---

[1] The use of the word in the LXX. Version of Psa. ii. seems, in the first instance, to have been merely a mistranslation resting on a false etymology of the word which in the Authorized Version is rendered "shalt break them." Here, however, and in Rev. xii. 5, as in so many other passages, the writer adopts the LXX. Version without any hesitation.

the disciples were tempted was an undue compliance with the customs of the Heathen as such. Their fear of offending them, their reluctance to confess before them that they were worshippers of the Crucified, was bringing them into bondage. And therefore they were told that he who resisted that temptation should take his true position, as being over those Heathen; should, in the great manifestation of the Kingdom, share in his Lord's rule of righteous, and therefore inflexible, severity; that then all the power and might of the Heathen that continued hostile to the Divine Kingdom should, like vessels of the potter not made to honour, be crushed to pieces.[1]

And, lastly, there was the yet more mysterious promise, "*I will give unto him the morning star.*" As with the manna, and with the fruit of the tree of life, so also here, that which the Lord holds forth as the supreme and crowning blessing is the gift of Himself,

---

[1] The argument used by Polycarp in dealing with the case already referred to presents a singular agreement with this passage: "Si quis non abstinuerit se ab avaritia [*i.e.* as above, πλεονεξία, in its secondary sense of impurity] ab idololatria coinquinabitur et tanquam inter gentes judicabitur. Quis autem ignoret judicium Domini? An nescimus quia sancti mundum judicabunt sicut Paulus docet."—(*Epist. ad Phil.* c. xi.)

the fruition of His glorious presence. The title of the "bright and morning star" is claimed by Him at the close of the Apocalypse as belonging to Himself as "the root and the offspring of David" (xxii. 16). And when He gives that star He gives Himself. Each symbol represents obviously a special aspect of that Divine presence. And the star had of old been the received emblem of sovereignty. Balaam had seen "a Star coming out of Jacob, and a Sceptre rising out of Judah" (Num. xxiv. 17); and the Magi of the East, seeing the star, set forth to worship Him who was born King of the Jews (Matt. ii. 2). It was the symbol of sovereignty on its brighter and benignant side, and was therefore the fitting and necessary complement of the dread attributes that had gone before. The King came not only to judge, and punish, and destroy, but also to illumine and to cheer. He was to be as the day-spring from on high, giving light to those that were in darkness and in the shadow of death (Luke i. 78). All lower gifts of prophecy or knowledge were but as one of the lights of earth, as lamp, or torch, or candle, shining in a dark and squalid place where they did but make the darkness visible (2 Pet. i. 19), but when the day-star (φωσφόρος, Lucifer, the light-bringer) should arise in their hearts, men would rejoice in the fulness of its radiance. The gift of the morning star is therefore the gift of that attribute of sovereignty no less than of its judicial and penal majesty. The conqueror in the great strife should receive light in its fulness and transmit that light to others—and so should take his place among those that turn many to righteousness, and "shall shine as the stars" for ever (Dan. xii. 3).

VI.

THE EPISTLE TO SARDIS.

THE REVELATION.

CHAPTER III.

1 AND unto the angel of the church in Sardis write ; These things saith he that hath the seven Spirits of God, and the seven stars ; I know thy works, that thou hast a name that thou livest, and art dead.

2 Be watchful, and strengthen the things which remain, that are ready to die : for I have not found thy works perfect before God.

3 Remember therefore how thou hast received and heard, and hold fast, and repent. If therefore thou shalt not watch, I will come on thee as a thief, and thou shalt not know what hour I will come upon thee.

4 Thou hast a few names even in Sardis which have not defiled their garments ; and they shall walk with me in white : for they are worthy.

5 He that overcometh, the same shall be clothed in white raiment ; and I will not blot out his name out of the book of life, but I will confess his name before my Father, and before his angels.

6 He that hath an ear, let him hear what the Spirit saith unto the churches.

VI.

IF the secular history of an Asiatic city had any legitimate connection with the interpretation of these Epistles, few names would offer a field of wider interest to the expositor than that ancient capital of the old Lydian monarchy through whose *agora* flowed the Pactolus with its golden sands; which was famed, in its remote past, at once for its manufactures and its coinage; whose name recalls the old tales, half mythical, half historical, of Gyges and of Crœsus. It preceded Miletus and Thyatira in the fame of its purple dye, and Corinth in that of its bronze, or compound metal known as *electrum*. Following in the track, however, of the method I have hitherto pursued, I cast but a passing glance at these external facts and seek rather to ascertain, as far as may be, what was its actual state at the time when the Apostle's mind was turned to its perils and its privileges, in his Patmos exile. The one event which then, probably, most influenced its condition was the great earthquake that had laid it waste in the reign of Tiberius (A.D. 17), and had been followed by a desolating pestilence. From this, however, the population had sufficiently recovered a few years later to be among the candidates for the honour of erecting a temple to the Emperor, who had then come to their aid; and at the time of the Apocalypse it was probably a fairly flourishing community. Its dominant worship, to judge by the ruins of the stately temple that still remain, was that of the great mother-goddess Cybele; and that worship, it will be remembered, with its eunuch priesthood and its orgiastic rites, was one which tended, as much almost as that of Dionysos or Aphrodite, to sins of a foul and dark impurity. In the midst of such a population, rescued from such a cultus, we have to think of the small community of disciples who were addressed, through their Angel, or Bishop, as the Church of Sardis.

Here, as before, we may well assume that the name by which the Lord reveals Himself at the opening of this Message—"*He that hath the seven Spirits of God*"—had a special bearing upon the state of the Angel and the Church to whom the Message was to be transmitted. The Spirit was thought of, to use the later terminology of the Nicene Creed, as the "Giver of Life" (τὸ ζωοποιὸν) and of all its sevenfold gifts; the seven Spirits of i. 4 and v. 6 were but forms of that divine life which He— one, yet manifold—imparted. These He, the Lord of the Churches, possessed and could call his own; for thus it is that He can "quicken whom he will:" thus He can impart the divine life, in all its marvellous variety, to those who stand in need of it. And He is also, as in the opening vision of the Seer, "*he that hath the seven stars,*" which represent the guides and teachers of the Church; He is able, that is, to bring together the gifts of life and the ministry for which those gifts are needed. If those who minister are without the gifts, it is because they have not asked for them. The union of the two attributes is, therefore, one both of encouragement and of warning. If each star shines with its peculiar radiancy, it is because it is under the power and influence of the seven-fold Spirit; if it has no life or light, and ceases to shine, there is the danger of its falling away from its place in that glorious band and becoming as one of the "wandering stars, to whom is reserved the blackness of darkness for ever" (Jude, verse 13).

And here both the warning and the encouragement were needed. Of the Angel of the Church at Sardis, and, by implication, of the society which he represented, it was said, "*Thou hast a name that thou livest,*"—hast the shew and the fame of a spiritual life—and yet thou "*art dead.*" The cause of that loss of vitality and strength is to be found, we may believe, in the absence, in this instance, of the "*tribulation*" and the "*endurance*" which were so prominent in the judgment passed on the works of other Churches. The members of the Sardian Church had not been tried in the fire of adversity; life had not been braced and strengthened by the conflict with persecution: men had been content with "*works*" of a lower and less noble kind, occasional acts of charity, the routine of decent conduct. There had been no open scandals; Sardis was still recognised by the other Churches as a living and true member of the great family of God, was even, it may be, winning their admiration for its seemingly energetic vitality. And yet the chill and the paralysis which were the forerunners of the end were slowly creeping in upon its life; death, not life, was already master of the position, the dominant characteristic of the Church as a whole, and of its spiritual ruler in particular.

To the Angel and the Church that was gliding into this state of spiritual torpor and death the command comes, "*Be watchful;*" *become* as one who watches (γίνου γρηγορῶν); rouse thyself, and stand as one who seeks to cast off that torpor. The words that follow present a singular diversity of reading—"*Strengthen the things that remain, which are ready to die*" (ἃ μέλλει ἀποθανεῖν; or, which *were* at the point to die (ἃ ἔμελλον); or, lastly, "*which thou wert at the point to lose*" (ἃ ἔμελλες ἀποβάλλειν). The meaning is, in all cases, substantially the same, but the best supported reading seems the second. In any case, the question meets us, What are those "things that are, or were, ready to die?" Are they those *members* of the Church in whom there were yet some signs of life, however feeble? or those *elements* of life, Christian graces and activities, which were not yet actually extinct? Both interpretations are, of course, grammatically tenable; but the distinct mention afterwards of persons as such, in the "*few names*" that are singled out for special praise, inclines the balance in favour of the latter. The Angel of the Church is called to wake up from his slumbers, and then to strengthen in himself the energy, the zeal, the love, the hope, the faith, which were so nearly dying out. In doing this he could not fail to help the persons also in whom this flagging of all spiritual vigour had been most conspicuous, or, in the language of the Epistle to the Hebrews, to "lift up the hands that hang down and the feeble knees" (xii. 12).

The reason for this command is then given. "*I have not found thy works perfect*" (literally, *not filled up* to the measure which God requires of thee) "*before God.*" And then, as in the analogous warning to the Angel of the Church of Ephesus (chap. ii. 5), there came other words: "*Remember, therefore, how thou hast received and heard.*" Personally it was an admonition to the Bishop of the Sardian Church to go back mentally to the time when he was yet a catechumen in the Christian Church, to recall the steps by which he then came under the oral teaching of apostles, or bishop-elders, how the traditions thus received in doctrine, ethics, discipline, had formed a complete and consistent whole — how, afterwards (here the change of tense, from the perfect to the aorist, points, it may be, to some definite epoch in his life, such as "the laying on of the hands of the presbytery" when he was consecrated to his ministerial office) he heard, in solemn words, what was the true pattern and standard of the duties of his office.[1] The counsel to "*keep*" all this is identical with that given by St. Paul to Timotheus, to "keep the good thing which had been committed to his charge" (2 Tim. i. 14), to "hold fast the form of sound words" which he had heard from his master "among many witnesses" (2 Tim. i. 13; ii. 2). In doing this, and in this alone, there would be the witness that he was indeed "*repenting*," not mourning with a fruitless regret over opportunities that had been lost and gifts that had been wasted, but entering on a new life with new impulses and new principles of action.

As in the Message to Pergamos, so here also, the exhortation is followed by a warning: "*Except thou watch, therefore, I will come as a thief, and thou shalt not know what hour I will come upon thee.*" Here, again, we have the language which we commonly associate with the great second Advent boldly transferred

---

[1] It seems right to mention the deeper meaning which Ewald gives to the words "thou hast received," as implying the reception of the gifts of the Holy Ghost. So taken they would appeal to an inward experience like that to which St. Paul appeals in writing to the Galatians (chap. iii. 2). I do not accept this as excluding the interpretation given above, but it is, perhaps, implied in the words "*how* thou hast received," stress being laid on the *manner*, the inward as well as outward accompaniments, of the instruction that had been imparted.

to some nearer and more immediate judgment. The very phrase, "*as a thief*," implies a reference to, and therefore the knowledge of, those "words of the Lord Jesus" in which, in connection with the self-same command to "*watch*," He had added, "This know, that if the good man of the house had known what hour the thief would come, he would have watched, and not have suffered his house to be broken through" (Luke xii. 39), and is, in fact, an echo of what, through those words, and the like teaching of St. Paul delivered to the Thessalonian and other Churches, had become a proverbial form of speech, that "the day of the Lord so cometh as a thief in the night" (1 Thess. v. 2). Dependent as this coming was on the state of the Sardian Church and its ruler, liable to be averted on renewed watchfulness and repentance, it must, of necessity, refer to the discipline, at once regulative and reformatory,—penal, yet not necessarily inflicting an irremediable penalty,—with which, in unlooked-for ways and at an unexpected season, the Lord would come upon the Church. Persecutions, distress, the open shame of being noted as a dead Church, exclusion from fellowship with other Churches, who should no longer recognise even its "*name*" to live—these should do their work, teaching all who were yet capable of being taught, warning others by the punishment of the hardened and impenitent.

In other Messages, as we have seen, first the good that exists in the Church is recognised, and then the evil that had mingled with it is marked out for censure. Here, unhappily, the evil was dominant, and the sharp words of rebuke had therefore to be spoken first. But the Judge of all the earth, then as ever, recognised and singled out for praise even the ten righteous men, if such there were, who had kept their integrity in the midst of a general corruption. "*Thou hast a few names*" ("names" for "persons," as in Acts i. 15, but with, perhaps, the underlying thought that He who speaks is one that "knows his own sheep by name," and looks on each in his own distinct personality) "*even in Sardis, which have not defiled their garments.*" The meaning of such an image lies of course on the surface. That which is to the spirit what the garments are to the body is the outward form of life which men behold, which in part expresses and symbolises the character, in part hides from view the nakedness of its personal life. Those, then, who had not defiled their garments were those whose outward lives had been free from impurity, who, in the analogous language of St. Jude, had kept that garment from being "spotted by the flesh" (Jude, verse 23). The same thought was, it is clear, symbolised in the practice of the early Church, possibly even a primitive practice, of clothing those who were baptized in white garments— the "chrisoms" of old English liturgical usage —as a witness of the purity of life to which their baptism pledged them. The parable of the man that "had not on a wedding garment" must have done something to fix this symbolism in the Apostle's mind, and this implied reference to that parable helps us there also to understand the true meaning of the symbol, and so to eliminate the more fantastic interpretations which see in it either the imputed righteousness of Christ or the outward ordinance of baptism.

The reward for this purity might seem at first to be the purity itself. They who have not defiled their garments are to "*walk*" with Christ "*in white*," for "*they are worthy.*" Here, however, it would seem, from the vivid pictures in chaps. vi. 11, vii. 9, 13, xix. 8, of the white robes given to the martyred saints, of those who were clothed with white robes which they had made white in the "blood of the Lamb," as if more than this were meant. The "white robes" are such "as no fuller on earth could whiten them," glorious and bright as those which the Apostle had seen on the night of the Transfiguration. In other words, as the reward of the pure in heart is that they shall see God, so that of those who have kept their garments from defilement is like in kind but more glorious in degree—a purity glorified and transfigured, pure even as He, their Lord, is pure (1 John iii. 3). Of that reward they are "*worthy*," and no dread of scholastic formulæ of "congruity" or "condignity" need hinder us from accepting the word in its natural meaning. There is a worthiness, a meetness, when the life prepares the way for the reward, and the reward is the completion and consummation of the life, which we need not shrink from recognising, as Christ Himself recognised it, and the very essence of which lies, in part, in the absence of any claim or consciousness of merit.

In this Message, and in this alone, the reward of him that overcometh is thus in part anticipated in what precedes it. If there is any difference, it is perhaps to be found in the use of the word περιβαλεῖται—he "*shall be clothed*," or "*shall clothe himself*," as denoting a more solemn investiture than the simple "*walking in white*." And looking to the fact of the obvious familiarity of the Evangelist with the prophecy of Zechariah, we can scarcely avoid seeing here a reference to the mysterious vision in which the High Priest Joshua, the son of Jozedek, stood face to face in conflict with Satan, the enemy and accuser, and, having overcome in that trial, had the fair mitre set upon his head, and was clothed in new raiment. (Zech. iii. 4, 5.)[1]

The reward, however, goes beyond this: "*And I will not blot out his name from the book of life.*" The words contain a whole mine of half-latent imagery. First we note the special appropriateness of the promise as given to those who were exceptions to the statement, too true of the greater part of the Church to which they

---

[1] I ought not to pass over, though I cannot altogether accept, Professor Lightfoot's interesting suggestion, in his Commentary on the Epistle to the Colossians (p. 22), that here, and in the parallel passage in the Message to Laodicea, there is a reference to the purple dyes for which both the cities, like Thyatira, were more or less famous. The image seems to me too natural and universal to require the assumption of any such direct reference. When we come to the description of those who had "washed their robes and made them white in the blood of the Lamb" (Rev. vii. 14), the case is, however, stronger. We can imagine the glance of the Apostle falling on one of the great dyeing vats used in the staple trade of the town, and seeing the linen garments steeped in the crimson fluid that looked like blood, and of his being thus led to think of those whose inmost life, steeped in the spirit of sacrifice of which the blood of Christ is the symbol, should emerge from that process, not "red like crimson," but, by the strangest of all paradoxes, "white as wool" (Isa. i. 18).

belonged, that "*they had a name that they lived, and yet were dead,*" whose names therefore would be blotted out of the book of life, which recorded only those of living members. The symbolism was one of the oldest in the Hebrew Scriptures, and occurring, as it does, for the first time in Exod. xxxii. 32 ("Blot me, I pray thee, out of thy book which thou hast written"), probably had its origin in the political life of Egypt. It was a natural expansion of the thought that one who was convicted of treachery or disloyalty to the State of which he was a member, should, as the preliminary step to the execution of the sentence of death or banishment, have his name struck out from the register of its citizens.[1] So in the fiery wrath of the 69th Psalm the extremest malediction is, "Let them be blotted out of the book of the living;" and this stands parallel with the clause, "Let them not be written among the righteous" (Psa. lxix. 28). So in Daniel's vision of the resurrection, those who were delivered out of tribulation included "every one that should

---

[1] Students of Greek history will remember the scene in which Critias, as the prelude to the condemnation of Theramenes, struck his name out of the list of the Three Thousand who could not be condemned except by a formal sentence of the Council.

be found written in the book" (Dan. xii. 1). To this image the Seer returns again and again. All should worship the Beast, except those whose names were written in the book of life of the Lamb (xiii. 3; xvii. 8). They only should enter into the holy city, the heavenly Jerusalem (xxi. 27). The words of the Message to the Church of Sardis are valuable as shewing that to have the name so written does not of itself secure, as by a divine decree, the indefectibility of perseverance. Of not a few it would be true, the very promise implying the warning, that their names, though they had been written in it, would hereafter be blotted out. The close of the Message comes as the natural sequel of this promise: "*I will confess his name before my Father and before his angels.*" Here we have in part the distinct echo of words which the Apostle had once heard from his Master's lips while He was yet on earth: "Whosoever therefore shall confess me before men, him will I confess also before my Father which is in heaven" (Matt. x. 32); or, as in Luke xii. 8, "before the angels of God." In the connection between this promise and the names that were written in the book of life we may trace, I believe, a probable reference to the strange Psalm of the Sons of Korah (Psalm lxxxv.), which appears to have been sung at some enrolment of proselytes from Egypt and Babylon, from Philistia and Tyre and Ethiopia, among the citizens of Zion. There also we read that when the Lord writeth up the people —takes, as it were, the census of the holy city— He shall rehearse, or count, uttering "as He counts" the names of those who were thus registered in what the Prophet Ezekiel, at a somewhat later date, calls "the writing of the house of Israel" (Ezek. xiii. 9).

VII.

THE EPISTLE TO PHILADELPHIA.

CHAPTER III.

7 AND to the angel of the church in Philadelphia write; These things saith he that is holy, he that is true, he that hath the key of David, he that openeth, and no man shutteth; and shutteth, and no man openeth:

8 I know thy works: behold, I have set before thee an open door, and no man can shut it: for thou hast a little strength, and hast kept my word, and hast not denied my name.

9 Behold, I will make them of the synagogue of Satan, which say they are Jews, and are not, but do lie; behold, I will make them to come and worship before thy feet, and to know that I have loved thee.

10 Because thou hast kept the word of my patience, I also will keep thee from the hour of temptation, which shall come upon all the world, to try them that dwell upon the earth.

11 Behold, I come quickly: hold that fast which thou hast, that no man take thy crown.

12 Him that overcometh will I make a pillar in the temple of my God, and he shall go no more out: and I will write upon him the name of my God, and the name of the city of my God, *which is* new Jerusalem, which cometh down out of heaven from my God: and *I will write upon him* my new name.

13 He that hath an ear, let him hear what the Spirit saith unto the churches.

VII.

THE city of Philadelphia, situated at the foot of Mount Tmolus, about twenty-eight miles south-east of Sardis, named after Attalus Philadelphus, King of Pergamos, and the centre of the wine trade of the region lying on the frontiers of Lydia and Phrygia, presented, so far as we know, the same phenomena of religious and social life as its nearest neighbours. There, too, there was a population mainly, of course, Heathen, but including at least three other elements distinct from it and from each other—Jews, Jewish Christians, and converts from Heathenism. What its spiritual condition was we gather from the Message, and from that only. Three facts connected with it may, however, be briefly noticed, as having some historical interest. 1. That, like Sardis, it had suffered severely from the great Asiatic earthquake in the reign of Tiberius. 2. That of all the Seven Churches it had the longest duration of prosperity as a Christian city, and is still a spacious town, with the remains of not less than twenty-four churches. 3. That of all the seven its name alone appears in the catalogue of modern cities. The meaning of the word,—" brotherly love," or "love of the brethren,"—perhaps also the special character of the promises connected with it in the Apocalyptic Message, commended it to the mind of William Penn as the fittest he could find for the city which he founded on the banks of the Delaware; and so it has won for the name of the old Asiatic city a higher niche of fame than it would otherwise ever have filled in the world's history.

The name by which the Sender of the Message here describes himself is that of "*the holy, the true, he that hath the key of David, he who openeth, and none shall shut; he who shutteth, and none shall open.*" Each of these epithets has a special significance and calls for a few words in explanation of it. 1. "*The holy.*" The word here used is, it must be remembered, ἅγιος, not ὅσιος, and represents the holiness of consecration rather than that which is ethical and indwelling. As such, in by far the great majority of instances, it is used either of the "saints" as consecrated, in spite of manifold individual weaknesses, to a life of devotion; or of the Temple and its sanctuaries, literal or spiritual, as dedicated to God's service (1 Cor. iii. 17; Ephes. ii. 21; Heb. viii. 2 and *passim*); more prominently still of the Holy Spirit, as sharing that otherwise incommunicable sanctity which belongs to the Divine Essence. Of the person of the Lord Jesus it is used but rarely. It would seem, however, to have been one of the names, more or less accepted as equivalent to that of the Messiah, which were current during His ministry. It came from the lips of the Gadarene demoniac when he uttered the cry, "I know thee who thou art, the Holy One of God" (Luke iv. 34). But it was not only from those lips that that word had come before in the hearing of the Apostle. If we take the reading of all the great MSS., including the Sinaitic, we find it was the form of the confession borne by St. Peter and recorded in John vi. 69: "Thou art the Christ," not as in our Version, "the Son of the living God," but, "the Holy One of God." That name is now recalled to the Disciple's mind in special connection, we may believe, with the memories of that day, but also, and more prominently, with the promises with which this Message ends, every one of which especially brings out the idea of consecration, the "*pillar in the temple of God*," the "*name*" and the "*city of God.*"

If textual criticism has helped us to trace the first of these great adjectives to its source, so, indirectly, it suggests the subtle links of association by which "*the holy*" and "*the true*" were connected. For it was on the self-same day that the beloved Disciple had heard from his Master's lips, for the first time, that word thus applied, when He spoke of Himself as "the *true* bread that came down from heaven." Whatever may have been its equivalent in the Aramaic which our Lord spoke, it is a familiar fact that the Greek word which St. John uses (ἀληθινός) was with him a favourite and characteristic one. It expressed, more than the simpler ἀληθής, "true with all the fulness of truth," true not only as opposed to false, but as distinguished from all shadows of, and approximations to, the truth. So we have, for example, the "*true* light" (John i. 9), "the *true* worshippers" (John iv. 23), the "only *true* God" (John xvii. 3). The last application has raised it almost to the level, not only of a divine attribute, but of a divine Name, and it is as such that it is used here. The Lord who speaks to the

Churches claims to be holy as the Father is holy, true as He is true.

In the words that follow we have a manifest reproduction of a passage in that strange episode in the prophecy of Isaiah (xxii. 15-25) which contrasts the character and the fortunes of Shebna the scribe and Eliakim the son of Hilkiah, that was "over the household" of Hezekiah. While the doom of shame and exile was predicted for the former, for the latter there was honour and advancement. "The key of the house of David will I lay upon his shoulder: so he shall open, and none shall shut; and he shall shut, and none shall open." His influence in the great crisis that was coming on the kingdom of Judah was to be mighty for good. He was to be "a father to the inhabitants of Jerusalem and to the house of David." Here, of course, the historical bearing of the words falls entirely into the background. And the words are chosen simply because they described, in terms which the prophecy had made familiar, that aspect of the highest sovereignty which was now most needed. They are not identical, it will be noticed, with those which described the Lord of the Churches as having the "keys of Hades and of Death" (chap. i. 19). There He was manifested as extending his sway into the world that lies behind the veil, the region of the unseen and spiritual, contemplated on its darker side. Here, in closer analogy with the promise of the keys of the Kingdom of Heaven to Peter (Matt. xvi. 19), what He claims is sovereignty over "*the house of David*," over the kingly palace of the Son of David, over the Church, as being the house of God. The right of admitting into that palace of the great King is his, and his alone. Others in vain attempt to admit when He excludes, or to exclude when He admits.

The next clause gives the more immediate application of the claim: "*I know thy works: behold I have set before thee an open door, and no man can shut it.*" As before, I take the words as spoken primarily of the Angel or Bishop of the Church in his personal character; and, secondly, of the Church so far as it was represented by him. So taken, we cannot doubt that the "*works*" which the Lord "*knew*" were such as He recognised as being worthy of all praise. And the context at once determines the nature of those works, and adds another link to the chain of evidence which shews that the teaching of the writer of the Apocalypse was, in all essential points, one with the teaching of St. Paul. If there was any phrase which more than another was characteristic of the language of the Apostle of the Gentiles, it was that of the "open door" which we are now considering. At Ephesus a "great and effectual door" was opened unto him (1 Cor. xvi. 19). At Troas a "door was opened unto him of the Lord" (2 Cor. ii. 12). He entreats those to whom he writes, to pray "that God would open to him a door of utterance to speak the mystery of Christ" (Col. iv. 3). So, in like manner, his friend and fellow-worker, St. Luke, records how that the Lord had "opened the door of faith unto the Gentiles" (Acts xiv. 27). In all these cases the open door refers to the admission of the Gentile converts into the great house of God, the widening opportunities for the mission work of the Church which the providence of God placed in the preacher's way. That phrase must, in the nature of things, have become current in the Churches which owed their very existence to the labours of St. Paul; and when it came to the ear and was recorded by the pen of St. John, it could not fail to recall the same thought and to signify the same thing. The words which came to the Angel of the Church of Philadelphia were accordingly of the nature of an assurance and a promise. He was encouraged to persevere in the work in which he had already laboured so well by the declaration that in this he was a fellow-worker with his Lord, that no narrowing exclusiveness, no bitter antagonism, should hinder its completion, that the door had been opened wide by Him who had " *the key of the house of David.*"

And this promise comes as a reward of faithfulness in the use of the opportunities that had already been granted: " *Because thou hast little power,*[1] *and yet didst keep my word, and didst not deny my name.*" The words point to something in the past history of the Church of Philadelphia and its ruler, the nature of which we can only infer from them and from their context. Some storm of persecution had burst upon him, probably, as at Smyrna, instigated by the Jews or the Judaising section of the Church. They sought to shut the door which he had found open, and would have kept so. They were strong, and he was weak; numbers were against him, and one whose faith was less real and living might have yielded to the pressure. But he, though not winning, like Antipas, the

---

[1] Not "*a* little strength," as in our English Version, which lays an undue stress on the substantive rather than on the adjective.

martyr's crown, had yet displayed the courage of the confessor, had kept the word, the doctrine, the creed, of his Lord, the mystery of the faith, the brotherhood of mankind in Christ, which was, in St. Paul's language, the substance of "the word of God," and had not been tempted to deny His name, the name of that Jesus to whom the Jews in their frenzy said, Anathema (1 Cor. xii. 3), through any fear of man. Like the faithful servant in the parable, he had thus been faithful in a very little (Matt. xxv. 23); and therefore, as the promise that follows shews, he was to be made "ruler over many things."

The reappearance of the same description as that which met us in the Epistle to the Church of Smyrna, points, as I have said, to the quarter from which the attack came. Here also we have those who "*are of the synagogue of Satan, that say they are Jews, and are not, but do lie.*" So far they seem to have gained the mastery. Though resisted, they are yet the stronger party. But the day of retribution is not far off. "*I will make them to come and worship before thy feet, and to know that I have loved thee.*" Before long, in that "*hour of trial which was about to come upon the whole world,*" in the storm of persecution which, springing from Heathen panic and suspicion, would involve both Christian and Jew alike, the man who had been faithful in his work would be courted as a protector even by those who had been his bitterest enemies. They would then bow down and do him homage, and would recognise, it may be in the outward events of life, it may be in the very fact that his power to protect them would flow from his influence with those Gentiles against whose admission they had so vehemently protested, that his Lord had "*loved him*," and would love him even to the end. He who had "*kept the word of the endurance of Christ*," the message which bade him endure, even as Christ also had endured the contradiction of sinners against Himself, the word which had passed, we may well believe, into a proverb, "He that endureth to the end, the same shall be saved," should, in his turn, be "kept" from that hour of trial or temptation, the "fiery trial" of 1 Pet. iv. 12, which was about to spread over the "*whole world*" of the Roman Empire, to "*try those that dwelt upon the earth.*"

And now, as before, in reference not only, or chiefly, to the far-off event that shall close the world's history, but to a nearer and more individual advent, we have the promise "*I come quickly.*" The trial should not be too long. The issue was not far off. Therefore "*hold fast that which thou hast,*" thy zeal, thy faith, thy endurance, thy open door, "*that no man take thy crown*"—that crown of life (Rev. ii. 10) and righteousness (2 Tim. iv. 8) which is reserved for the faithful combatant. The promise to him that overcometh is, however, in this instance, more definite, and, if one may so speak, more appropriate, than the simple crown of the conqueror: "*I will make him a pillar in the temple of my God, and he shall go no more out; and I will write upon him the name of my God, and the name of the city of my God, the new Jerusalem, which cometh down out of heaven from my God, and my new name.*" The circle of imagery into which we are here brought anticipates the more wonderful and glorious visions with which the Apocalypse closes. There also we hear of "the great city, the holy Jerusalem, descending out of heaven from God" (Rev. xxi. 10). But there are differences of detail in the terms of the promise here which call for notice, and are, each of them, singularly suggestive. (1) In the vision of the holy city the Seer beheld no temple in it, for "the Lord God Almighty and the Lamb were the temple thereof" (chap. xxi. 22). That which constitutes a sanctuary in the highest sense of the word temple (ναός) is the presence felt and, it may be, seen, of the god to whom it is dedicated. So our bodies are "temples (ναοί) of the Holy Ghost" (1 Cor. vi. 19). So the Lord Jesus spake of the "temple of his body" (John ii. 21). But in that heavenly city (itself, when we analyse it, but the symbol of a reality which as yet we know only in part and through types and shadows) that divine Presence is everywhere manifesting itself to the whole company of the blessed according to the capacity of each; and just as the material universe, in its relation to the creative power and the permanent and immanent energy of the Creator as sustaining it, is the temple of the Lord God Almighty, so, where there is the presence of the Lamb, one with the *Logos*, revealing the Fatherhood and redeeming love of God, there also is the Temple which is wherever that presence is. Here, however, in the earlier stage of the symbolic apocalypse, the mind of the Seer was not as yet ripe for that thought. It is to come to him when he *sees* the city. So long as he hears of it only by the hearing of the ear, he is to picture it to himself as having a temple analogous to that of the earthly Jerusalem, with which he was familiar. And in that

temple he that overcame was to be made
"*a pillar.*" It will be remembered that that
was a title which, in its relation to the Church
of God, had been borne by the Apostle himself.
He, with Cephas and James, had been among
those who seemed to be "pillars" of the
Ecclesia at Jerusalem (Gal. ii. 9), sustaining
the fabric of its polity. And now he hears the
gracious promise that, as he had been in the
earthly Ecclesia, which was the Temple of the
living God, so should every one that overcometh
be in that heavenly Temple. And that position
once gained should never afterwards be forfeited.
"*He shall go no more out.*" Here on earth there
is to the last the possibility of failure. The
surest guide may wander from the right path.
The pillar may give way, and need removal,
that the fabric may remain unshaken.[1] But
there the victors shall abide for ever, each,
under this aspect of the symbol, a column in
the Infinite Temple, as each, under another
aspect, had been as a "living stone" in the
structure of the temple upon earth. He that
had the keys of the house of David would close

[1] It is just possible that there may here be a local reference to the earthquakes from which Philadelphia had suffered, and which may have so shaken the fabric of many of its temples that some, at least, of their pillars had to be removed and new ones erected in their place.

the gates upon those who were received into the Holy City, so that there should be no departure.

"*I will write upon him the name of my God.*"[1] So, in chap. xxii. 4, we read of the servants of God in the heavenly city that "his name shall be on their foreheads," and in chap. ix. 4 of those "who have the seal of God upon their foreheads." We can scarcely fail to see in this promise a reference to the thin plate of gold which was borne upon the forehead of Aaron and his successors in the office of the High Priest, and upon which was to be graven, "like the engraving of a signet, HOLINESS TO THE LORD" (Exod. xxviii. 36). And so the promise takes its place side by side with those which speak of the elect of God as being, like their Lord, sharers in a kingly priesthood. Their life of consecration, their fulfilment of the priestly ideal on earth, will hereafter be recognised by the consummation of that life in the heavenly Temple in which they have been made as pillars, not mute and motionless like the

---

[1] It has been a question whether the "writing upon *him*, or *it*" (the Greek admits, of course, of either rendering), refers to the pillar as such, or to the man as represented by it. Probably the frequent use of human figures in the caryatides of Greek temples suggested the identification of the two.

columns in human form of an earthly temple, but living, moving, worshipping.

"*And the name of the city of my God, which is New Jerusalem.*" Were the thoughts of the Seer directed here, also, to the prophetic symbolism of the past, or does the mystery of the new name belong entirely to the far future, unrevealed to him and therefore hidden from us? An interpreter may well shrink from speaking over-boldly in answer to that question; but, on the whole, the analogy of the symbolic imagery of the Apocalypse generally suggests the conclusion that the key of the mystery is to be found in that volume of the Prophets which was to St. John so inexhaustible a storehouse. The new name might be that which meets us at the close of the prophecy of Ezekiel, as the name of the renewed and glorified city which he saw in vision, "*Jehovah-shammah*"—"the Lord is there" (Ezek. xlviii. 35). More probably, as it seems to me, both because the name itself is of deeper and richer significance and because the Messianic prophecies of Jeremiah, connected as they were with the proclamation of the New Covenant (Jer. xxxi. 31), were more prominent in the thoughts of men than those of Ezekiel, we may think of "*Jehovah-tsidkenu*"—"the Lord our Righteousness"—which was, we read in Jer. xxxiii. 16, to be the name of the city in its glorified and transfigured state, no less than of the Anointed King, as in the more familiar words of Jer. xxiii. 6. Every inhabitant of that celestial city would count it his glory to have that name written upon his forehead, the sign of that completed citizenship in heaven (the πολίτευμα ἐν οὐρανοῖς of Phil. iii. 20) which had been his joy and comfort upon earth.

Last and greatest in the list of names which the Conqueror is to bear as the insignia of his victory is the "new name"[1] of the Lord Himself. Here we are reminded of the analogous promise to the Church of Pergamos—the "new name," though not in that instance of the Lord who speaks, but of the disciple who has been faithful to the end. There we saw that the new

---

[1] I am unwilling to pass over without notice a suggestion which I have received from a friend, the Rev. W. Reid, of Edinburgh, as to the "new name" of the Lord Jesus which is here brought into prominence. Adopting a true inductive method of inquiry, he has asked himself whether the Apocalypse itself contains any characteristic name or title that had not been used before or applied to Christ. And he finds the answer in the fact that the Greek word Ἀρνίον, "the Lamb," is so used in not less than twenty-eight passages in this Book, and not elsewhere. The name is raised to a co-ordinate rank with that of God (Rev. vii. 10; xiv. 4); the Church is the Lamb's bride (Rev. xxi. 9); the Twelve are the Apostles of the Lamb (Rev. xxi. 14). So used, the Name gathered up into itself the humiliation and the glory, the sacrifice and the exaltation, the meekness and the gentleness of Christ, and became in very deed a Name which is above every name.

name was the symbol of a new and transfigured character, and this may guide us to a right apprehension of the meaning of the promise here. The name is not one that is merely "*new*" now, but one that shall be new in the day of the final victory. It is, therefore, more even than those two great names, the "Word of God" and "King of kings and Lord of lords" (chap. xix. 13-16), which the Apostle heard and beheld in one of his later visions. For these his own writings made familiar to the minds of men even during the time of struggle and incompleteness, and there was, besides these— written, it would seem, not, like the latter of those two names, on "the vesture and the thigh," but on the diadems that crowned his brow—another more mysterious name, seen but not understood even by the Seer, a name "*which no one knoweth but himself.*" Full and rich as are the names of Jesus now, the Son of God, the Son of Man, the Word, the Christ, the King of kings and Lord of lords, revealing what we can in some measure even now comprehend and realise, there will be in the completed glory of the kingdom a yet fuller revelation of all that He is in Himself, of all that He has been to us. Now "we know in part, but then we shall know even as also we are known; now we see through a glass darkly, but then face to face" (1 Cor. xiii. 12). We know not what we shall be, but we know that we shall be like Him, for we shall see Him as He is; and that knowledge will find its adequate expression, as before, in a Name. And that Name written on him that overcometh will mark him not only as a citizen of the heavenly Jerusalem, but as the subject, nay, rather, as the heir of the Eternal King.

VIII.

THE EPISTLE TO LAODICEA.

THE REVELATION.

CHAPTER III.

14 AND unto the angel of the church of the Laodiceans write ; These things saith the Amen, the faithful and true witness, the beginning of the creation of God ;

15 I know thy works, that thou art neither cold nor hot : I would thou wert cold or hot.

16 So then because thou art lukewarm, and neither cold nor hot, I will spue thee out of my mouth.

17 Because thou sayest, I am rich, and increased with goods, and have need of nothing ; and knowest not that thou art wretched, and miserable, and poor, and blind, and naked :

18 I counsel thee to buy of me gold tried in the fire, that thou mayest be rich ; and white raiment, that thou mayest be clothed, and *that* the shame of thy nakedness do not appear ; and anoint thine eyes with eyesalve, that thou mayest see.

19 As many as I love, I rebuke and chasten : be zealous therefore and repent.

20 Behold, I stand at the door, and knock : if any man hear my voice, and open the door, I will come in to him, and will sup with him, and he with me.

21 To him that overcometh will I grant to sit with me in my throne, even as I also overcame, and am set down with my Father in his throne.

22 He that hath an ear, let him hear what the Spirit saith unto the churches.

VIII.

THE position of Laodicea, on the banks of the Lycus, within a short distance of Hierapolis and Colossæ, brought the Church of that city within the range, if not of the direct influence of St. Paul's personal teaching, at least of that of those who had been taught by him, and of an Epistle specially addressed to it. If we accept the words of Col. ii. 1 in their natural meaning, the members of that Church were as dear to his heart and filled him with as profound emotion as any could do who had not "seen his face in the flesh." To them, from his Roman prison, he had sent a letter, probably by the same messenger that carried the Epistle to the Colossians. (Col. iv. 16.) The question whether it was a letter exclusively for them, or that which we know as the Epistle to the Ephesians, considered as an encyclical letter to the Asiatic Churches, and reaching them in due course, is one which we need not now discuss. It will be enough to remember that a letter written at the same time as those to the Churches of Ephesus and Colossæ would, probably, in the nature of things, treat of the same subjects and be written in the same tone. Those to whom it was addressed would learn to think of Christ as of One in whom dwelt "the fulness of the Godhead bodily" Col. ii. 9; in whom, "in the fulness of time, all things were to be gathered together, both which are in heaven and which are on earth" (Ephes. i. 12), as the "head of all principality and power" (Col. ii. 10)

The names by which the Message to the Angel of the Church of Laodicea was ushered in were accordingly such as reminded him of the truths that had been thus proclaimed by the great Apostle of the Gentiles: "*These things saith the Amen, the faithful and true witness, the beginning of the creation of God.*" It need hardly be said that this is the solitary passage in which the word, so familiar as a formula of emphasis even in the Greek version of our Lord's teaching, so familiar also in the worship of both Jews and Christians, appears as a personal name claimed by the Lord Jesus as His own. It is obvious that as it came to the inner ear of the disciple it must have thrown back his mind, full, as it was to overflowing, of the words of the prophets in their old Hebrew speech, upon the passage in which Isaiah had spoken of the new name of Jehovah as the God of Truth (*Elohim-Amen:* Isa. lxv. 16). But with this there may also have come the recollection of the very syllables in which his beloved Lord had declared Himself to be "the Truth" (John xiv. 6), lingering in his memory as that of "Ephphatha" and "Talitha cumi" did in the memory of those from whose reports St. Mark compiled his Gospel, and leading him to see new meanings in the old familiar words. To him it had now come to be equivalent (as in the LXX. version of the passage in Isaiah) to the word which he elsewhere uses in Gospel and Epistle, for the True ($\dot{o}$ $\dot{a}\lambda\eta\theta\iota\nu\dot{o}s$), as standing, not only in conjunction with words such as the true Light, the true Bread, or, as here, the true Witness, but absolutely as in 1 John v. 20. It is not without interest to remember that the language of the Pauline Epistles had already presented an approximation to a like use, and that in Christ the promises of God were Yea, and in Him Amen (2 Cor. i. 20).

To some, however, among his readers that new name was likely to be an obscure and hard saying, and for them, therefore, after his manner elsewhere,[1] he adds the Greek equiva-

---

[1] As in the case of Siloam (John ix. 7); Gabbatha (xix. 13); Golgotha (xix. 17); the Devil and Satan (Rev. xx. 2).

lent of the Hebrew name: "*the faithful and true witness*," and thus they were led to the first proclamation of that Name, with all that it involved, in the opening words of the Apocalypse (chap. i. 5). Both the words are thus brought together, we may believe, because the Message that was to follow was one of sharp reproof and condemnation. Men were to remember that Truth had its severer as well as its more gracious aspect, and that He who was the "faithful and true witness" of the everlasting love of the Father would cease to be faithful unless He also testified against the sins of men, against the lukewarmness and indifference which were shutting out that love. And to this there is added the higher and more mysterious title, "*the beginning of the Creation of God*." Here we find another striking instance of that to which I have endeavoured throughout this volume to give its due prominence,—the identity, in its great broad outlines, of the teaching of St. John and of St. Paul. For not only does the name express the self-same truth as the "first-born of every creature" in Col. i. 18, but the very name, the Beginning ($\dot{\eta}$ $\alpha\rho\chi\dot{\eta}$), appears in the best MSS. as thus applied in Col. i. 18 in connection with "the first-born from the dead;" and we can hardly doubt, from its use here, that it had passed into the liturgical and devotional phraseology of the Asiatic Churches of the valley of the Lycus. The stress laid in the Epistle to the Colossians on the inferiority of those to whom the self-same name of ἀρχαὶ was given in the other sense, of all "*principalities* and powers" (Col. i. 16, ii. 15), to the One who was the true Beginning, or, if we might venture on an unfamiliar use of a familiar word, the true *Principality* of God's creation, may account for the prominence which the name had gained, and therefore, for its use here in a Message addressed to a Church exposed, like that of Colossæ, to the risks of angelolatry, of the substitution of lower principalities and created mediators for Him who was the Head over all things to his Church.

In the absence of other information we can only gather the state, outward or inward, of the Church of Laodicea from the words that follow. It is probable from what we know of the city in which the Church was found, that it was exposed, more than most other Churches, to the temptations that come from wealth. The trade of the town, mainly that of dyeing, which it shared with Thyatira and with Sardis, was prosperous; and almost alone of the Asiatic cities it was able, without any subvention from the

Imperial treasury, to recover from the effects of an earthquake which, in A.D. 60 (according to the view I have taken, but a few years before the date of the Message sent to it), had laid many of its buildings low. We can well believe that not a few of the converts to the faith of Christ belonged to the wealthier class, even as we find at Ephesus that there were those who were "rich in this world" (1 Tim. vi. 17). And the temptation which then, as ever, riches brought with them was to take things easily, to enjoy life and the pleasures which wealth can buy; to act practically on the rule, "*Surtout, point de zèle*," when that zeal brought with it the necessity for self-denial or exertion. The love that had once been warm or glowing was waxing cold, though it had not as yet passed into open apostasy and antagonism. The Angel, or representative leader of the Church, had shared in this general declension, and to him, therefore, the rebuke is primarily addressed: "*I know thy works, that thou art neither cold nor hot.*" The meaning of the latter word (the Greek of which occurs here only in the New Testament) lies, of course, on the surface. It denotes the temper of *fervent* love, a love that warms and animates the whole life, the temper, we must remember, specially characteristic of the Apostle who records the Message. In him there had been, at first, the fiery zeal that marked him out as one of the Sons of Thunder, and made him seek to call down fire from heaven to consume the village of the Samaritans; and this, though it had been purified, had not lost its old intensity, and equally in the actual language of the Epistles (2 John, verses 10, 11; 3 John, verses 9, 10), and in the tradition of his fleeing from the presence of Cerinthus,[1] we trace the ardent spirit that alike loves strongly and strongly hates. The precise spiritual state described as "cold," is, we may well believe, the exact opposite of this. It is not an equal fervour on the side of falsehood and of evil, not an open hostility to the truth, the fanaticism of the heathen and the heretic. The temper of St. Paul was not "cold" when he led the persecution against Stephen. It is simply the entire absence of any love to Christ and his cause, of even the least enthusiasm for any

---

[1] The tradition referred to is given by Irenæus (iii. 3) as received by him from Polycarp, and is to the effect that the Apostle, in his old age, entered the public bath at Ephesus, and found there Cerinthus, the leader of those who denied that the Son of God had come in the flesh. On seeing him he rushed out of the building, before taking his bath, and said to those who were with him, "Let us flee from this place, lest the building fall upon us, for Cerinthus, the enemy of the truth, is there within its walls."—(Euseb. H. E., iii. 28).

person and any cause, an absence which, in the former case, may be the result of simple ignorance, or, as in Matt. xxiv. 12, of the presence of an abounding iniquity. The condemnation of that state is expressed in terms which startle us by the naked boldness of the imagery employed: "*I would thou wert cold or hot: so, because thou art lukewarm, and neither hot nor cold, I am about to spue thee out of my mouth.*"

That "*tepid*" temperature (not of cold passing into heat, but of heat passing into cold) was that which has as its physical effect (in the case *e.g.* of water) the sickening sense of nausea, and which in its moral aspect causes in most earnest minds a loathing that is not roused by the state described as "cold." That feeling has, in not a few cases, found its analogues in human utterances. Men prefer an entire stranger to the "candid friend." The profession of a dispassionate attachment to institutions, ecclesiastical or political, is often felt to be but the prelude to desertion or betrayal. The language of the great poet of mediæval Christendom singles out for sharpest reprobation those who were—

"*A Dio spiacenti ed a' nemici suoi.*"[1]

---

[1] It may be worth while to give the whole passage. I quote from an unpublished translation :—

"Speech, many-tongued, and words of dire lament,
  Language of sorrow, accents of despair,

And the reason lies, it is clear, in the tendencies of such a state to self-satisfaction and, therefore, self-deceit. The man who has no religious feeling at all may be roused to penitence—conscience may be awakened, and the work of conversion may begin. But the "lukewarm" state is for the most part that which is blind to its own shortcomings. It is unreal, and sickly, and yet thinks that it is in a true and healthy state. As Mr. Carlyle has somewhere put it, in one of those epigrams that haunt one's memory, "it is the hypocrisy which does

---

>   Deep voices hoarse, and hands in anguish bent,
>   These made a discord through the dusky air
>   Which ever floats eternally the same,
>   As whirls the sandstorm driven here or there.
>   And I, upon whose brain strange wonderings came,
>   Said, 'Master, what is this that now I hear,
>   And who that race whom torment so doth tame?'
>   Then he to me : 'This wretched doom they bear,
>   The sorrow-smitten souls of those whose life
>   Nor foul reproach nor glorious praise did share :
>   Mingled they are with those who in the strife
>   Of angels were nor rebels found nor true,—
>   Apart withdrawn when wars in Heaven were rife.
>   Heaven, fearing loss of beauty, spurned that crew ;
>   Nor were they ordered to the depths of Hell,
>   Lest to the damned some glory should accrue.'
>   *   *   *   *
>   At once I understood and saw full clear,
>   These were the souls of all the caitiff host
>   Whom neither God nor yet His foes could bear."
>   DANTE, "*Inferno.*"

not know itself to be hypocritical." And it needs therefore words of sharp warning and rebuke from Him who searcheth the hearts and reins, or from any who, having the mind of Christ, can speak, as He would have spoken, of this inner baseness. It may be noted, as tending to confirm the assumption that the Gospel of St. John and the Apocalypse were the work of the same writer, that this is the fault which in the former, again and again, he notes for special condemnation. Those who could not believe are less the object of his censure than those who, believing, feared to confess the Christ " lest they should be put out of the synagogue, for they loved the praise of men more than the praise of God " (John xii. 42, 43). Something of the same feeling is seen in the language of the Epistle to the Hebrews, as to those who "forsake the assembling of themselves together," who need therefore to be " provoked to love and to good works," lest there should remain for them only "a certain fearful looking for of judgment and fiery indignation" (Heb. x. 24, 27).

The underlying grounds of the condemnation, the secret working of this tepidity of the soul, are brought before us in the words that follow: *" Because thou sayest, I am rich, and have become* wealthy, and I have need of nothing, and knowest not that thou" (the pronoun is emphatic in the Greek, as is also the article) "*art the wretched and the pitiable one, and poor, and blind, and naked.*" It is clear that the imagined wealth here is that of spiritual, not temporal, riches. In regard to the latter the boast would probably have been true, and would have called for no such stern contrast. And yet it is not the less true that it was the possession of the riches of this world that made the Laodicean Angel and his Church so satisfied that they had the riches of the other. They took the "unrighteous mammon," not only as a substitute for the "true riches," but almost as a proof that they possessed them. Outward ease and comfort took the place of inward peace; prosperity was thought a sure sign of Divine approval. We cannot read the history of the Church of Christ, or look around us, or retrace our own experience, without feeling that it has often been so, both with churches and individual men. Lethargy creeps over them; love is no longer active: material success, multiplied endowments, the power of giving money as the one embodiment of love to God or man,—these have been the precursors of decline and of decay. On the larger scale it has been found hard to rouse to energetic spiritual action a Church that was threatened with no dangers, resting on an arm of flesh, secure in the State's support. On the smaller it is equally hard to convince a respectable and well-to-do Christian that he can be wanting in the true wealth of love when he is ready, on occasion, to draw a cheque for a charitable institution.

The state described was bad, but it was not hopeless. The great Healer has a word of advice even here, and the advice, though not without a touch of irony, would not have been given in the mere scorn of indignation: "*I counsel thee to buy of me gold tried in the fire, that thou mayest be rich: and white garments, that thou mayest be clothed, and that the shame of thy nakedness be not made manifest: and anoint thine eyes with eye-salve, that thou mayest see.*" The tone of irony, of which I have just spoken, will be felt, I think, in that advice to "buy," given to one who has just been pronounced a beggar where he fancied himself rich. Where can he find the price for these inestimable treasures? The answer to that question is to be found in the words of Isaiah, which this counsel at once calls to our remembrance, "Ho, every one that thirsteth, come ye to the waters, and he that hath no money; come ye, buy, and eat; yea, come, buy wine and milk without money and without price" (Isa. lv. 1). And yet the irony contains in both instances the truest and most gracious tenderness. The wine and the milk, the gold and the white garments, are beyond all price, as measured by earthly standards, and therefore they are *given* freely. And yet, on the other hand, they have, in some sense, their price. The man forsakes his earthly treasure that he may have treasure in heaven. St. Paul counts the things that had been as his "gain," his fancied spiritual riches, as "loss" for the excellency of the knowledge of Christ Jesus his Lord (Phil. iii. 7, 8). Lastly, besides this renunciation of unreal wealth in both its aspects, there is a price which even the beggar can pay, when he has found that it will be accepted by the Lord who is so ready to sell. He can give *himself*—can yield his body, soul, and spirit, to be dealt with as his Lord shall see fit, if only he may receive the priceless treasure which he needs. To accept that discipline is the counsel now given, and it is implied that it will not be without a sharp severity. The "gold" which Christ will thus "sell" to him who seeks it, the treasure of holiness and peace and joy, is that which has been "*tried in the fire;"* and this, as in all like cases, implies chastisement and suffering. The "*white garments*" that hide the shame of nakedness, the true holiness of life which alone prevents the exposure of that "inner vileness" of which even the saints of God are ever painfully conscious, are those which have been made white in the blood of Christ, which symbolises suffering. The eye-salve, which gives clearness of vision, does so (one may refer, if such a reference be needed, to the history of Tobit's recovery from his blindness—Tobit x. 8-12) not without the pricking smart that clears away the blinding or beclouding humours.

Of the three forms of discipline thus indicated, the first scarcely needs any discussion here; the second has been dealt with in speaking of the Message to the Church of Sardis; the third is new, and stands almost, if not altogether, alone in the imagery of Scripture, and calls therefore for a few brief notes. I know not whether the suggestion which I am about to make has been made by any other interpreter, but most readers will, I think, answer in the affirmative, if asked whether they remember anything in St. John's Gospel of which these words remind them. They will recollect how, in one instance at least, our

Lord gave sight to the blind, not by word or touch only, but by the use of an eye-salve, or *collyrium*, how "he spat on the ground, and made clay of the spittle, and *anointed* the eyes of the blind man with the clay" (John ix. 6), and they will not think it strange to assume that these words must have recalled to the mind of the Seer what he had thus himself witnessed in one, if not many, instances (comp. Mark viii. 23). The very state of the Laodicean Church had indeed been described in words recorded in connection with that very narrative: "If ye were blind, ye should have no sin: but now ye say, We see; therefore your sin remaineth" (John ix. 41). As in those cases, sight came through that which derived its power to heal from the lips of Christ, so here that which would remove the spiritual blindness was the Power of that Divine Word which would make the man's inward eye see himself as God sees him, and with the smart of that knowledge draw forth tears of penitence which, as they flowed, would cleanse.

The end of the Message stands out in striking contrast with the beginning. No other opens with such sharp unsparing severity; no other closes with such yearning tenderness and a promise so exceeding glorious. Something there was, we know, in the character of the beloved Disciple, as seen in his Epistles and the traditions connected with his name, which corresponded to that combination of qualities that seemed at first hardly compatible. But that something was but the reflection of the union of the two in the Lord and Master, into whose likeness he had grown. Where the highest love is, there must also be severity, and the severity is a proof of love, yearning, pitying, and seeking to restore. And so, after piercing as with the sharp two-edged sword to the dividing asunder of soul and spirit, of the joints and marrow, He, the Lord of the Churches, in the gracious words that follow, pours in the oil and the wine that are to cleanse and heal: "*As many as I love I rebuke*" (*i.e.* rebuke so as to convict),[1] "*and chasten. Be zealous, therefore, and repent.*" There is in the Original a force which it is not easy to reproduce in a translation. The "*I*" stands first, and has the special emphasis which always attaches to the presence of the Greek pronoun. It is as though he suggested a contrast between himself and others. "Human friends may seek simply to please and soothe, to speak smooth things and prophesy deceits;

---

[1] The word is the same as that which describes the office of the Comforter (John xvi. 8).

but not so with Me. I give a far other proof of love, and so deal with those who are dear to Me as to make them conscious of the evil that mars their peace and keeps them from their true blessedness; and when that consciousness has been roused, I bring them under the loving, though it may be sharp, discipline of chastisement." The command, "*Be zealous, therefore, and repent,*" may seem at first to invert the natural order of the soul's recovery. Must not "repentance," the turning from evil, precede the righteous zeal which is to animate the true life? In some cases, perhaps in most, that is, doubtless, the natural order. But the inward life of the soul, in all its subtle workings, cannot always be brought under these sharply-defined formulæ; and here we can, I think, recognise a special adaptation to the exigencies of the case with which the great Healer was dealing. The root-evil of the Laodicean Church and its representative was their lukewarm indifference, the absence of any zeal, of any earnestness. And the first step, therefore, to higher things was to pass into a state in which those elements of life should no longer be conspicuous by their absence. "*Be zealous;*" let that be (so the tense of the Greek verb indicates) the true and abiding state; and then (the tense changing to that which indicates a thing done once for all) let the first act of that new state be to throw itself with all its force on the side of God, to repent of the evil of the past, and to enter on a new course of action for the future.

And then we come to that which Christian art and poetry have alike made familiar to us— the promise that speaks of the love which rebukes and chastens, the love of the divine Friend in all its infinite tenderness: "*Behold, I stand at the door and knock: if any man hear my voice and open the door, I will come in to him, and will sup with him, and he with me.*"

The words of the promise that thus come as the sequel to the rebuke are referred by most commentators to the imagery of the Song of Solomon, and are claimed accordingly as sanctioning the mystical interpretation of that Book. There the bride tells her tale of expectancy and joy, "I sleep, but my heart waketh; it is the voice of my beloved that knocketh, saying, Open to me, my sister, my love, my dove, my undefiled" (Song Sol. v. 2); and the frequent recurrence of that image in the visions of the Apocalypse—the "marriage supper of the Lamb;" the "New Jerusalem coming down as a bride adorned for her hus-

The Epistle to Laodicea. 211

band" (Rev. xxi. 2), the "bride, the Lamb's wife" (xxi. 9)—seems at first to give a high degree of plausibility to the view that it is to be found here. I am constrained, however, by what seems to me a true method of interpretation, to reject that view and to seek for another meaning. It cannot be too strongly impressed on our minds that wherever that image of the Bride and the Bridegroom occurs, either in the Old or the New Testament, it shadows forth the relation of Jehovah to His people as a collective unity, of Christ to his Church. The wider the induction the more convincing will be the proof that, however largely the other idea may have prevailed in the writings of Christian or other Mystics, this, and not the relation of the individual soul to its Maker or Redeemer, is throughout Scripture the truth shadowed forth in all bridal and nuptial parables. But here the promise is distinctly personal, and describes, under whatever figure, that which belongs to the living individual experience of a joy with which a stranger doth not intermeddle. There is no picture here of the bride tarrying for her spouse. That which is brought so vividly before us is the arrival of a guest at night, of a guest who comes to cheer and guide and comfort. And if so, is it altogether an idle dream to imagine that St. John may have had other sources of imagery open to him than those which he found in books, however sacred; that the memory of his own early years may have been brought back to him by the words that he now heard, as supplying the fullest expression of his Lord's communion with the loving and trusting soul? Remember how his discipleship had begun by his tarrying where the divine Friend was for the time dwelling, invited by the words, "Come and see," and there listening during the long hours, till day passed on into evening and evening into night (John i. 39). Remember how, in all likelihood, he was sharing in the same high blessedness in the lodging at Jerusalem, when Nicodemus came to Jesus by night, and so was able to record that marvellous teaching as to the new birth which he alone reports, and reports with such a vivid fulness as to make it hardly possible to doubt that he himself had heard it (John iii. 2–13). Think of the three years of companionship growing into ever closer and closer friendship, so that he became known to all men as "the disciple whom Jesus loved," of the long-continued intimacy implied in the words which led that disciple to take to his own house the sorrowing mother of his Lord, and then ask whether such a scene as that which this verse brings before us may not often have presented itself in his own actual experience? Think of the day's work over, the sick healed and the poor taught, and then the Master, after His manner, leaves the shouts of the crowd and the stir of the town, and withdraws into some solitary place to hold communion with His Father; and the scholar remains in his lonely chamber in the cottage at Bethsaida, or the lodging at Capernaum, watching, not sleeping, waiting for the return of Him in whose presence he found life, postponing till then the simple meal with which the day habitually closed. And then, as he watches, there is the distant sound of footfall, and then He, the expected Friend, stands at the door and knocks, and then the voice, so familiar in its gentle sweetness, though capable also of the tones of stern rebuke, tells him who it is, and then he rises, and the door is opened, and the Friend enters. The Son of Man, who had not where to lay His head, finds shelter under His disciple's roof: He comes, first, as a guest, and sits down to sup with the scholar, who thus, as a host, receives Him; but soon the places are changed, and He takes, as it were, the place that of right belongs to Him. He blesses and breaks the bread and gives thanks over the cup of wine.

He is now guest no longer, but the host. The disciple "sups with him."[1]

This I take to be the outward framework of the parable of this verse, at once probable in itself, and a more adequate representation of the spiritual truths shadowed forth than any bridal imagery. What men want is the consciousness of the presence of a friend that "sticketh closer than a brother." It is better (the very devotional utterances which express the opposite feeling being themselves the strongest proof of it) even for women, in their individual personality, to think of Christ as the friend and the brother, rather than as the bridegroom and lover of their souls. And now the promise that this blessedness shall belong to any one who will but claim it—even to one who had been "wretched, and miserable, and poor, and blind, and naked"—is given in all its fulness. There is something, we cannot doubt, in the inner life of every one who is zealous and repents which answers to the several stages of the experience that was thus brought home to St. John's memory— Christ "stands at the door and knocks." Warnings come that either rouse us from our slumbers, or fall on the expectant ear and make us feel

---

[1] The words remind us also of a like figurative promise in Luke xii. 37.

that the Judge who rebukes and chastens is not far off. Suffering in one or other of its many forms, unexpected judgments, or unlooked-for mercies, these tell us that He is asking for admission. If we listen in the attitude of reverence and faith we "hear the voice," become more distinctly conscious of that Presence, not as the Judge only, but as the Friend who comes to plead with us and for us, and so to be our Advocate and Comforter. Well for us if then we open the door of our hearts to Him, even though it may have been long barred against Him, and the weeds that creep over it may shew Him how little we have been prepared to give Him entrance. For then it shall be true of us also, that while we receive Him, He, on His side, is receiving us. If we invite Him to share what we have to offer Him of that which has been indeed His own gift to us, He, in His turn, will call us to His own heavenly feast, and so even the poor chamber of our hearts will become thus honoured and glorified by His presence, as one of the "many mansions" in "the house of his Father."

These thoughts serve at least to prepare the way for the glorious words with which the Message to Laodicea closes: "*He that overcometh, to him will I give to sit with me in my throne, even as I also overcame and am sat down with my Father in his throne.*" It is, as I have said, the highest and most glorious of all the promises with which the Seven Messages end. It speaks of nothing less, if we may use a familiar word in a new sense, than the *apotheosis* of the conqueror. So, when on earth, the prayer of Jesus for His disciples had been for nothing less than this, " As thou, Father, art in me, and I in thee, that they also may be one in us ; " and He had said of them, " The glory which thou gavest me I have given them," and therefore He could pray, " Father, I will that they also, whom thou hast given me, be with me where I am " (John xvii. 21-24). The conquerors in the strife with evil share " the throne of God and of the Lamb," the throne which is the great centre of all the visions of the wider future that from this point begin to unfold themselves to the prophet's gaze (Rev. iv. 2 ; xxii. 1, and *passim*). They are, in some sense which we cannot as yet fathom, made " partakers of the Divine Nature " (2 Pet. i. 4), sharers in the holiness, the wisdom, and the love, and therefore in the glory and the majesty which have been from everlasting.

And so the Messages to the Seven Churches close. I have not attempted in dealing with them to dwell at any length on the history of these Asiatic cities in the past, or on their present state, in some instances of decay and desolation, in others of an outward prosperity, under the yoke of their Mahometan conquerors. Whatever interest may attach to such descriptions they contribute little or nothing, I believe, to a true interpretation. Still more absolutely have I thought it right to exclude what has been called the "prophetic" interpretation, which sees in the Seven Churches, as in the seven trumpets and the seven seals, the symbolism of an historical sequence, and connects each with some one period, more or less clearly marked, in the history of the Universal Church, beginning with the apostolic age and ending with that which followed on the Reformation. I entirely agree with Archbishop Trench in looking on such a method of interpretation as grasping at the shadow and losing the substance, as leading to fantastic and arbitrary applications of divine words, and robbing them, in so doing, of all their interest and life. But it remains true, as I trust these notes have not failed to shew, that however directly historical and personal in the first instance, these Messages have, for that very reason, a wider range. Any Church, at any time, may look into these pictures of spiritual excellence or decay as into a mirror, and see in one or other of them its own likeness. The soul of each individual disciple may learn to behold in them his own besetting temptations, the rebuke or the encouragement which he himself most needs, the rewards to which even he may rightly and reverently aspire.

THE END.

www.ingramcontent.com/pod-product-compliance
Lightning Source LLC
Chambersburg PA
CBHW021831230426
43669CB00008B/936